P9-AFT-646

the great Philly Cheesesteak book

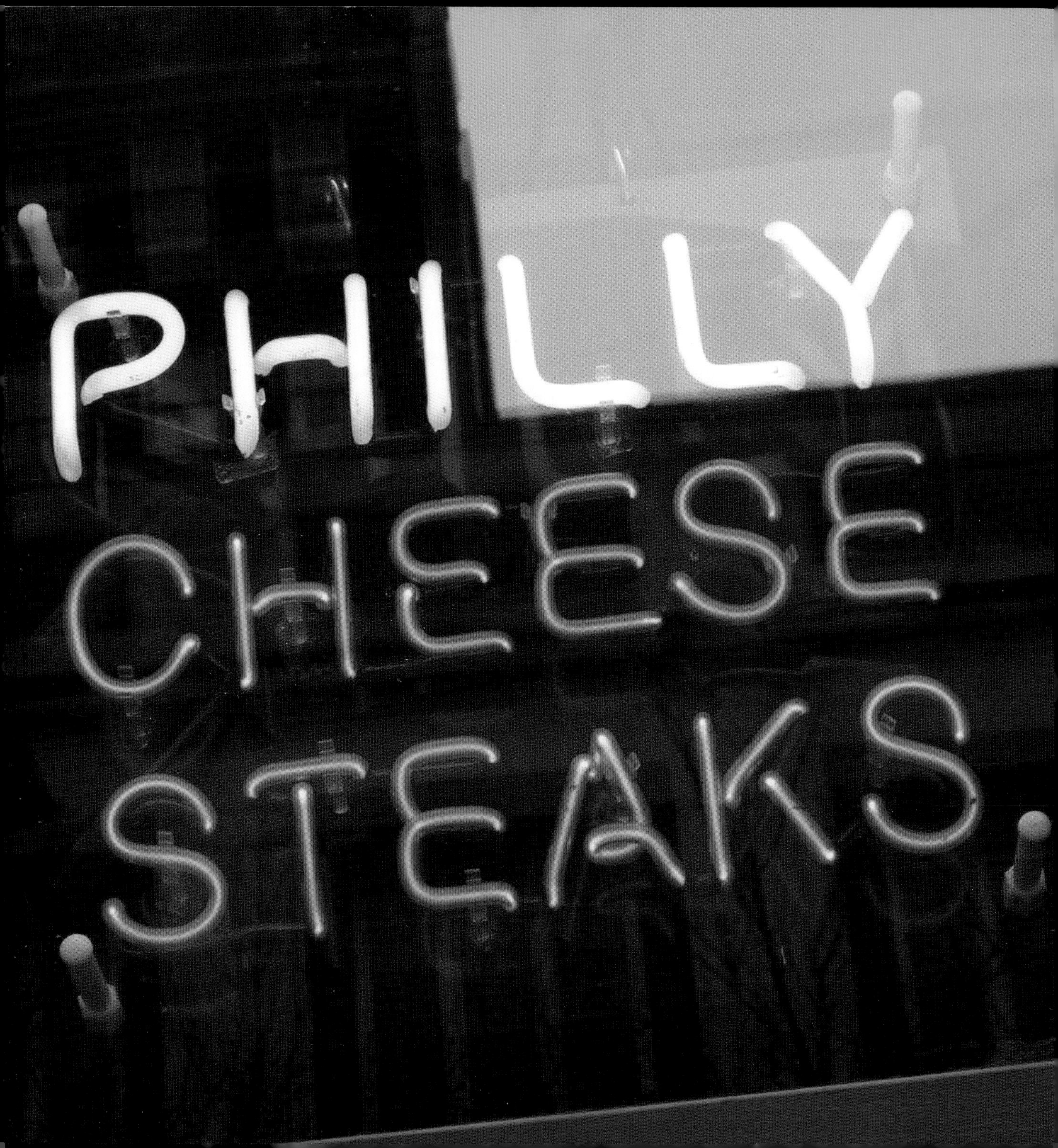
PHILLY
CHEESE
STEAKS

the great Philly Cheesesteak book

Carolyn Wyman

RUNNING PRESS
PHILADELPHIA · LONDON

Copyright © 2009 Carolyn Wyman
All rights reserved under the Pan-American and International Copyright Conventions
Printed in China

This book may not be reproduced in whole or in part, in any form or by any means, electronic or mechanical, including photocopying, recording, or by any information storage and retrieval system now known or hereafter invented, without written permission from the publisher.

9 8 7 6 5 4 3 2 1
Digit on the right indicates the number of this printing

Library of Congress Control Number: 2008943525

ISBN: 978-0-7624-3547-0

Design by Joshua McDonnell
Edited by: Geoffrey Stone
Typography: Albadi, Archer, Cooper, Helvetica

Running Press Book Publishers
2300 Chestnut Street
Philadelphia, Pennsylvania 19103-4371

Visit us on the web!
www.runningpresscooks.com

PERMISSIONS AND CREDITS

All text and photos by Carolyn Wyman except for the following photographs (or specified illustrations or recipes), for which grateful acknowledgment is made. Photos by Shirley Fonner: Cover bottom second from right; 13 (original courtesy Rick Olivieri); cover bottom third from right, 15, 16, 33 top right, and 150 (originals courtesy Pat's King of Steaks); 36; 40; 47 top; 48; 56 (original courtesy Fran Dalessandro Sack); 58; 59; 60 top; 62; 84; 85; 138; Back flap author photo by Philip L. Blumenkrantz; p. 14: Temple University Libraries, Urban Archives, Philadelphia, PA; p. 19: Michael S. Wirtz/Philadelphia Inquirer; p. 20: ©AP Images; p. 32 (left): ©AP Images/Jacqueline Larma; p. 32 (right): ©Emmanuel Dunand/AFP/Getty Images; p. 29 (top left) and 33 (left and bottom right): Geno's; p. 39: Campo's; p. 43 and 45 (left): Joseph Groh/Chink's; p. 51: Cosmi's Deli; p. 61: Starr Restaurants; p. 67 (top): Grey Lodge Pub; p.71 (bottom): Photo by Philip L. Blumenkrantz; p.73 (left): Tony Pearlingi; p. 76: John Danze/Johnny's Hots; p. 83 (graphic): Courtesy The Beef Checkoff; p. 87 (top): Leo's Steaks; p. 90: Shipon's Steaks; p. 118: Talk of the Town; p. 121: Photo by Greg Anderson, courtesy of the Food Research Institute, University of Wisconsin-Madison; p. 124: Tony Luke Jr.; p. 129: Herr's (The Herr's name and logo are registered trademarks of Herr Holdings Inc. and are used under license. © 2008 Herr Holdings Inc.); p. 130: Gaglione Bros.; p. 131: Courtesy CKE Restaurants, Inc.; p. 132: Vincent Casciato/Colonial Corner; p. 133: Ono Cheese Steak; p. 134: Sherri Abbulone/Joey's Famous Philly; p. 135: Pop's Philly Steaks, Las Vegas, Nevada; p. 137: Steak

Escape; p. 139: Billadelphia's Authentic Philly Foods; p. 140: Photo courtesy Hamburger Helper (Hamburger Helper is a registered trademark of General Mills, Inc.); p. 141 (right): Courtesy of Nestlé USA, Inc.; p. 141 (left): Tat's; p. 142 (Express Cheesesteaks text): Mickey Jou; p. 146: Rasta Imposta (Photo by Stuart Goldenberg.); pp. 148-149: David Neff/Neff Associates; p. 151: Tony Luke Jr.; p. 152 (graphic): Andrew Stein; p. 153 (right): ©AP Images/NBCU Photo Bank; p. 155 (recipe): Pat's King of Steaks; pp. 156-7: Ten Speed Press, Berkeley, CA (www.tenspeed.com) (Recipes for Italian rolls and biga reprinted with permission from The Bread Baker's Apprentice by Peter Reinhart. © 2001 by Peter Reinhart.; p. 157 (right recipe): Fran Dalessandro Sack; p. 158 (recipe ((with Albert Paris)) and photos): David Neff/Neff Associates; p. 159 (cheesesteak soup recipe): Courtesy Campbell Soup Company; p. 161 (recipe): Czerw's Kielbasy, Philadelphia; p. 163 (recipe and photo): Four Seasons Hotel, Philadelphia (Photo by Cliff Mautner, Cliff Mautner Photography); p. 165 (cherry pepper dressing recipe): Dimitri's International Grille; pp. 165-6 (Philly Cheesefake recipe): Elizabeth Fiend (www.bigteaparty.com); p. 166: Photo by Allen Fiend; pp. 166-167 (cheesesteak empanadas recipe): Jessica O'Donnell/Good Dog Bar; pp. 167 (Schmitter® recipe and schematic): McNally's Tavern: © 2008 H&J McNallys Tavern Inc. All rights reserved. Used with permission. Schmitter® is a registered trademark of McNallys Tavern, Inc.; p. 168 (photo): Eugene Gagliardi Jr./Visionary Design. Steak-umm is a registered trademark of the Steak-Umm Company, LLC.

for **Philip Greenvall,**

One top-quality prime, U.S.-raised, aged friend

Table of Contents

ACKNOWLEDGMENTS

Most Philadelphians would rate their steak shop visits as among life's greatest pleasures. It was likewise a chief pleasure of putting together this book. But running a stand or restaurant that makes a great cheesesteak is demanding work, which is why I am grateful for the time steak business owners and managers named in these pages took to tell me their stories and pose for or provide me with pictures. Special thanks are due to those who submitted to multiple visits and phone calls, especially Frank Olivieri Jr. and Sr. of Pat's, Joey and Geno Vento and Diana Vergagni of Geno's, Abner Silver of Jim's, Alexandro Apsis and Fran Sack of Dalessandro's, Rose Marchese of Big John's and Perry Walton of Pop's and bestcheesesteaks.com.

The history chapter of this book also greatly benefited from conversations with Maria Anna Olivieri and Evelyn Olivieri-Cirello and books by South Philadelphia historian Celeste Morello (especially *The Philadelphia Italian Market Cookbook* and *Philadelphia's Italian Foods),* the work of journalists who have covered the Philadelphia food scene since the 1930s, and the librarians at the Philadelphia Free Library, Temple University's Urban Archives and Philadelphia Media Holdings who helped me find those old photos and stories (particularly Michael Panzer, Frank Donahue and Brenda Galloway-Wright).

My understanding of the elements that make up a cheesesteak was greatly enhanced by conversations with John Karamatsoukas and James Trivelis of the Original Philadelphia Cheesesteak Company and Gene Gagliardi Jr. of Visionary Design, as well as Bill Irwin and Don Howe of Devault Foods, Harry Ochs of the Reading Terminal Market, Steve Altieri of A. Altieri & Sons and Harry Crimi of Cappuccio's Meats (meat); Dan Pisanelli Sr. and Jr., Peter Reinhart and Charles Mallowe Jr. of Amoroso's (bread); and Bill Wendorff of the University of Wisconsin and Basil Maglaris of Kraft Foods (cheese).

The Cheesesteak Abroad chapter was founded in experiences and opinions of the sometimes named, sometimes anonymous habitués of the Phillyblog, Egullet, Roadfood and Chowhound Web sites. Help on how to order a cheesesteak in other languages came from Flavio Frontini, Cat Lee, Marta Amour, Helen Hwang, Ed Dixon, Jan Fertig, (the single) Nima Dejbod and his "assistant," Joe Foote, Paul Kunkel, Ashwini Jambhekar, Susanne Fusso and Irina Aleshkovsky; with special thanks to WRDW 96.5 FM's Chio in the Morning for the wonderful idea.

Others providing research or other help, leads, valuable information and/or their valuable time include Ed Weiner, M.J. Fine, Juan Linares, Peter Kubilus, Paul Runyon, Kathleen

Pierce, Barbara Traisman, Sal Grande, Madeleine Morel, Signe Wilkinson, Bill DeAngelis, Tom Wethern, Joel Spivak, Ed Beckerman, Julia Zagar, Ruth Snyderman, Shea Dunn, Sylvia Petalino, Jane Auspitz, Joe Pie, Elizabeth Fiend, Ralph Gagliardi, Louise Chakejian, John Faulkner and Chrissy Eckert of the Campbell Soup Co., Pam Becker of General Mills, Roz O'Hearn and Marie Olson of Nestle, Marlene Frusco of Frusco Steaks, Joe Marchesani of Garrett Hill Pizza, John Connell and James Bryant of Lee's Hoagie House, Voula Karamitopoulos of Philly's Phatties, Mike McGravey of Duff's Steaks, Chris Hashem of John's Pizza, Corie Moskow of Gloss Public Relations and Brian Wilson of Le Castagne.

Mickey Jou and Shirley Fonner are the first people I ever entrusted with significant research and photo help, respectively, on one of my books and they won't be the last based on the great work both of them did.

That shouldn't be surprising considering that I met Mickey and Shirley through colleagues at Philadelphia *City Paper*: Thanks to Pat Rapa, Reseca Glasser and Mike Regan for providing those links, to Carolyn Huckabay and Brian Howard for time off as the deadline pressure began to build like a bubbling cauldron of covered Whiz, and M.J. Fine (again!), Joel Tannenbaum, Gail Kennedy and Maria Moeller for subbing so competently for me while I was steak-engaged.

And of course, this would be just a manuscript and not a book were it not for the smart folks at Running Press, including Geoffrey Stone, Josh McDonnell, Kristen Wiewora, Greg Jones, Jennifer Kasius and Jon Anderson; copy editor Jennifer Greenstein, photo researcher Susan Oyama, and James Gregorio, the literary lawyer that brought us happily together.

I think of James as just the newest member of the Wyman kitchen crew headed by the beloved Philip Blumenkrantz (who lent his car, camera and stomach to this project) that also includes Joyce Morral, Thelma Warenda, Marge Rosenblum, Ginger Restemeyer, Maya Lea, Tami Fertig and Helen Hwang.

To them and all the other friends, family and colleagues who lent support by giving me space: It's time to collect on your free cheesesteak.

INTRODUCTION

Philadelphia is the birthplace of American democracy, the U.S. flag, the public library, the post office, the mint, the stock exchange, the hospital, and the computer. But Philly's greatest gift to American society could well be the cheesesteak.

Eating this sandwich is among the top three things tourists want to do in Philadelphia, according to top tourism Web site gophila.com—right up there with visiting the Liberty Bell and Independence Hall. But unlike visiting these national landmarks, eating cheesesteaks is also an activity locals enjoy with regularity. Seventeen percent of Philadelphians eat this sandwich at least once a week (4 percent get a daily fix), according to a 2006 poll conducted by the Global Strategy Group for *Philadelphia* magazine. And when locals are not eating cheesesteaks, they're talking about them. Philly food discussion boards are filled with heated debates about the best stands and endless esoteric discussions about steak-making techniques (Should the meat be served in whole slabs or chopped? Topped with Whiz or provolone? Scooped off the grill with a spatula or the open roll?) In fact, *Philadelphia Inquirer* restaurant critic Craig LaBan calls cheesesteaks "*the* single food Philadelphians care about most passionately"—more than hoagies or anything served at LaBan's top-rated restaurants.

So important are cheesesteaks to the local identity that they are regularly exploited in local advertising (as in Sprint Nextel wireless's "coverage like steak on cheese" billboard campaign), employed as metaphor ("as Philly as a cheesesteak"), and used as part of local political strategy (see page 32 for how John Kerry learned this the hard way).

Why is the cheesesteak so popular? And why has it grown in popularity both nationally and locally when so many other foods that were invented here (pepper pot soup, for instance) have all but disappeared? The fact that it's a portable food at a time when nobody has time to sit down for meals could be one reason. The simplicity, affordability, and familiarity of its basic ingredients could be another. What American doesn't like bread, beef, and cheese? But the real key is the way these ingredients come together to create this different and delicious eating experience. In fact, the cheesesteak flavor is so distinctive and widely appealing that it's become a standard flavor variation for a wide variety of supermarket foods (see chapter 3) and a standard item on the menus of chains like Applebee's, Johnny Rockets, and even Hooters, where they are enjoyed by people from everywhere *but* Philadelphia.

Philadelphians think it's impossible to get a good cheesesteak more than sixty miles outside of the city. Pennsylvania governor and cheesesteak lover Ed Rendell once explained to a group of postal union convention delegates in 2006 where the outland cooks go wrong: "First, they use good meat. You need the fattiest, stringiest meat to get a proper taste. The second mistake is, they use real cheese. Real cheese doesn't melt like Cheez Whiz. And third, when they fry their onions, they actually drain off the grease. You can't do that." He was partly kidding, though fat *is* one of the major building blocks of great taste.

Still, the biggest surprise of months of visiting steak stands for this book was how little obvious grease most of their cheesesteaks displayed. Out of more than forty steaks, there were probably only half a dozen that called for the famous "Philly lean"—that is, holding the steak out in front of you so all the grease falls on the ground instead of on your shoes and clothes.

I actually think the real reason you can't get a great cheesesteak outside of Greater Philly is that no one cares more about this food than Philadelphians. And a great cheesesteak is as much about the place that sells it, the people who serve it to you, and how and why they do what they do as it is about the actual food. That's a lot of what I hope to capture in this book's largest chapter, which profiles local cheesesteak restaurants.

Some say cheesesteaks are so popular in Philadelphia because they are the food embodiment of Philly's unsubtle, sloppy, and in-your-face populace. The typical Philly steak shop owner is likewise unpretentious and honest to the point of rudeness. You would probably never be admonished for ordering incorrectly at a McDonald's, as you might be at Pat's, but then you probably don't remember your last McDonald's visit—nor is it likely that anyone working there remembers you. I'd rather have my existence acknowledged—even if it's just to be yelled at!

And as much fun as I've had working on this book, I do expect some real unpleasantness to come with its publication. Where does a native New Englander of English, Welsh, and French-Canadian descent who has only been regularly eating cheesesteaks for the five years she's been a Philadelphian get off writing *The Great Philly Cheesesteak Book*? Despite my qualifications as the author of a biography of the equally unhealthy Spam, I expect to hear questions like that as well as complaints about my stand selections. In response, all I can say is (1) there are seventy-five hundred restaurants in Philadelphia, most of which serve cheesesteaks; and (2) I am ready for you with pen in hand—hopefully some of these other wonderful places will make it into a future edition.

I expect there also will be those who will argue from the other side of the counter that cheesesteaks are unworthy of book-length attention, being a dated and clichéd representation of the eating habits of a city that now has much healthier and more sophisticated eating options. But today's cheesesteak purveyors are keeping up with the times with their chicken, vegetarian and gourmet offerings (some featured in this book's recipe chapter).

In fact, Georges Perrier, the owner of Le Bec-Fin in Philadelphia, which *Food & Wine* magazine once called this country's finest French restaurant, recently helped judge a local cheesesteak contest with apparent pleasure. Yes, the Whiz has seeped into the culture and character of this city and, increasingly, this country—very, very deeply.

THE ENVELOPE, PLEASE

This book is not a contest and I don't have enough years of cheesesteaks coating my artery walls to qualify as a cheesesteak expert. Still, after visiting more than forty steak shops and tasting their wares, it's hard not to have an opinion about what makes a great cheesesteak.

The roll must be superfresh, obviously, and soft but not flabby—like Conshohocken Bakery's and Liscio's. The cheese should be noticeable but not overwhelming, which is why I am beginning to understand so many stands' preference for American over Whiz or provolone. And, what is perhaps the hardest thing to find, the beef should taste like beef and have the chew of steak without being tough or gristly. The onions should neither be raw nor so caramelized as to resemble ketchup. And all four of these ingredients should be balanced—no one component should dominate.

What shops came closest to my ideal on the days I visited? For slab-style (as opposed to chopped and my preference), Johnny Hots, Donkey's, Grey Lodge Pub, Philips, Talk of the Town, and Sonny's; for chopped, Claymont, Dalessandro's, and Pagano's. And before you throw this book across the room, remember that I am also a Spam fan.

CHAPTER 1:
THE STEAK STORY

MAKE OR SELL A PARTICULAR FOOD FOR A LIVING—NO MATTER HOW GOOD—AND THERE COMES A POINT WHERE YOU HOPE TO NEVER SEE OR SMELL THE STUFF EVER AGAIN. SO IT WAS WITH PHILADELPHIA HOT DOG VENDOR PAT OLIVIERI ONE DAY IN 1930. "HOT DOGS AND FISH CAKES; FISH CAKES AND HOT DOGS; THAT'S ALL I EVER EAT. HERE," PAT SAID, HANDING SOME CHANGE OVER TO HIS YOUNGER BROTHER, HARRY. "GO DOWN TO THE BUTCHER AND GET ME SOME THIN-SLICED STEAK."

Harry got the steak and Pat fried it up on his hot dog grill, along with some diced onions he had on hand for the hot dogs, put it on a hot dog bun, and then, just as Pat was about to take his first bite—darned if a regular customer, a cabdriver, didn't show up and interrupt. "Whatcha got there, Pat? Smells good—how much?"

The question stopped Pat. He hadn't been planning to sell the sandwich so had no price in mind. But business wasn't so good that he could afford to turn down a sale. "Five cents and we got a deal," Pat shot back in at least one version of the story. Others say he charged ten cents or asked for nothing but the cabby's opinion, which was extremely positive.

And thus, in circumstances that rival the invention of rubber and corn flakes in both flukiness and import, the steak sandwich got its start.

"Whatcha got here, Pat? Smells good—how much?"

Those whose knowledge of Philadelphia begins and ends with fourth grade history lessons about George Washington, John Adams, and Thomas Jefferson probably think of that city as being primarily inhabited by the WASP descendants of English bluebloods. In fact, Philadelphia was shaped and enlivened by waves of immigration both before the American Revolution (by the Swedes, Germans, and Irish) and after (when Russians, Chinese, and Southern blacks came). Pat Olivieri's parents were part of the five million Southern Italians who immigrated to America between 1880 and 1920, and specifically part of the two hundred thousand Italians who settled in South Philadelphia between 1890 and 1930. Most

Pat serves up a sandwich in one of the oldest surviving pictures of his stand.

of these Italian Philadelphians were farmers escaping high taxes and exhausted soil. But Pat's dad, Michael Olivieri, had a good job running the local public transportation agency in Chieti, the capital city of Abruzzi's Chieti province, until the rise of Mussolini. Michael's connections were on the wrong side of the political breeze and he did not want to see his sons fight for a cause he didn't believe in, so he packed his family off to Philadelphia.

As with other immigrants before and since, Michael Olivieri found his high standing and relative prosperity in his old country of no consequence in the new. Unable to speak English and and bearing a "funny" name, he faced as much discrimination and difficulty getting a job as the ex-farmers. He actually sent his wife, Maria, and seven children (Dominic, Carmella, Louis, Pat, Nicholas, Frank, and Harry) back to Italy for a time until he got a job on the docks in 1923. Sixteen-year-old Pat stayed in Italy a while longer with an uncle to finish his schooling. But in America, Pat's college degree only got him a drop forger job at the city's Flexible Flyer sled factory. Too smart and ambitious to be satisfied with only a factory job, Pat bought a hot dog cart and began working it as a side business with the help of brother Harry.

Hawker and peddler jobs were favorite occupations of new immigrants in Philadelphia and it's easy to see why: they didn't require a big capital investment or entail getting hired by someone from a different and more established ethnic group. Pat was also smart in his choice of spots—in front of a horse water trough at a time when horses were still a mode of transportation and at a trolley stop at the northern edge of the largest collection of food shops and stands in South Philadelphia. (Remember, this was a time when ice box refrigeration required multiple shopping trips each week, if not every day.) Among those stands were street vendors selling sandwiches made with hearty Italian bread (from one of dozens of neighborhood bakeries), tripe, and other low-grade pieces of meat (some just meat juice!) that were cheap and filling and so perfectly suited to those tough Depression times.

But despite the suitability of Pat's wares, his great location, and his steak sandwich innovation, Pat's stand wasn't

The Route 47 trolley ran right through Pat's Italian Market neighborhood.

an immediate, runaway success. Shortly after finally quitting Flexible Flyer to work the stand full-time, Pat actually returned to the factory to ask for his job back. His third wife, Evelyn Olivieri-Cirillo, recalls, "But on his way to see the boss, so many of his former coworkers came up to him to congratulate him on the new stand and getting out of there that he left without doing it."

It was just the first of many hero's welcomes Pat was to receive during his lifetime and easy to understand, given what kind of guy he was. "He was exciting. People loved being around him," says Evelyn.

"He was a true showman," says great-nephew Frank Olivieri Jr., who, as an inheritor of Pat's King of Steaks business, is a beneficiary of that showmanship.

Many people think cheesesteaks became famous because of their taste. But every day, in shops across America, hundreds of delicious sandwiches get made and eaten that are never heard about in other places. No, the cheesesteak became famous because of Pat.

Pat in his crowded, late 1930s' kitchen.

Singer Tony Bennett (left) with Pat

Sam Spade (aka Humphrey Bogart) playfully sticks it to Pat.

"He was not the kind of guy who wanted to be stuck behind a grill all day," says Maria Anna Olivieri, the daughter of Pat's brother Harry, the guy who ended up behind the grill while Pat ran around to local theaters and nightclubs to create interest in his business. Pat would deliver free steak sandwiches to the stars and get them to pose for pictures that he hung from the walls and ceilings of his stand. (Black-and-white 8 x 10 photos from the time, many still posted at Pat's, show Pat with Louis Armstrong, Benny Goodman, Humphrey Bogart, Jimmy Durante, and even Sabu the Elephant Boy.) Then Pat would invite the celebrities back to the stand for more, sometimes even driving them there him-self in the big red Cadillac he acquired once his marketing efforts began to pay off. And entertainers did come, in part, because from the time it opened through the 1970s, Pat's was one of the only places still open and serving food after 10 p.m. in Philly.

A rumor that Pat's steaks were made of horsemeat—supposedly started by one of Pat's competitors and believable in a time of meat rationing—would have been the ruin of many a food business. But it just spurred Pat into one of his greatest publicity stunts. Going to the newspapers, he announced that he would pay the then-enormous sum of $10,000 to anyone who could prove the horsemeat claim. People swarmed the stand to search the trash cans and, of course, buy steaks to see for themselves. Frank Jr. believes Pat actually started the rumor himself to increase business. And when interest in the contest began to wane, Pat gave the story fresh fuel with his well-publicized purchase of a horse stable.

Although initially Pat's competition was limited to stands in the immediate area trying to cash in on his overflow (including Joe's, Mike and Carol's, and Jimmy's, the latter owned by the father of current Pat's rival Joe Vento), from the mid-1940s to the mid-1950s, steakeries inspired by Pat's success began popping up in other neighborhoods and the nearby suburbs—Chink's in the Northeast, Jim's and Larry's in West Philly, Mama's in Bala Cynwyd, and Donkey's in Camden, New Jersey, among them. By that time, Pat had become almost as much of a celebrity as the entertainers he had previously courted. His every move was big news, although admittedly, a lot of what Pat did *was* big—like purchasing the thirty-six-room Chateau of Dreams mansion in Wynnewood, which Pat renamed Villa Olivieri. The 1960 birth of Robin, Pat's daughter with Evelyn, also made all the papers along with the news that she had two teeth and therefore was "ready to eat steak."

Pat had opened a second stand at Thirty-third and Dauphin in 1938, and on July 22, 1951, a *Philadelphia Inquirer* story about the opening of a companion sit-down restaurant right across the street marveled at its 400 seats and $2,800

Part of a neon and porcelain enamel sign that once adorned Pat's Strawberry Mansion restaurant from the mid-1950s on. The crown now decorates one wall of Jack's Firehouse Restaurant in Philadelphia's Fairmount section.

Current keepers of the Pat's Steak flame: Frank Olivieri Jr. (left) and Sr.

(see page 85 for one such story)—and it's hard to say for sure with so many shops then in the steak-making business—the Olivieris say it was the late "Cocky" Joe Lorenzo. His motivation was the same that led Pat to invent the steak sandwich in the first place. Sick of eating the shop's hot dogs, fish cakes, and steak sandwiches, Joe ran home one day in the early 1950s to grab a cheese sandwich, brought it back to Pat's, and then got the eureka notion of placing some of the American cheese on top of a hot steak. Harry's son, Frank Sr., later added the provolone and Cheez Whiz—the latter was particularly prized because employees didn't have to wait for it to melt, which allowed Pat's by-then quite long lines to move more quickly. Frank Sr. explains the shop's unusual tradition of putting slices of cheese on the bread instead of on the meat on the grill (as Lorenzo did it and as most other shops still do) as rooted in his desire to keep milk and meat products separate for Jewish customers. (See What's Wit the Whiz on page 120 for more on cheesesteak cheese.)

By the late 1950s, Pat had handed off most of the day-to-day running of his shops to Harry and his other brother Louis so Pat could pursue real estate deals and manage boxer Harold Johnson (see page 20). With Evelyn's two daughters from a previous marriage to help raise, Pat didn't have much time to hobnob with celebrities anymore. Not that it really mattered. By then, entertainers, politicians, and tourists came of their own accord. *American Bandstand* and the *Mike Douglas Show*, both produced locally, kept the city stocked with celebrities from the mid-1950s to the late 1970s. Comic Don Rickles talked about the place frequently on Johnny Carson's *Tonight Show* and native son David Brenner showed up at the shop to make steaks and get the place some free publicity. Pat

crystal chandelier as well as its proprietor's wardrobe (150 custom-made suits, 500 pairs of slacks, and 40 pairs of shoes) and habit of buying himself a new car every year.

Pat and his brother Harry were also generous to others. Mary Lorenzo, wife of longtime Pat's employee Joe Lorenzo, recalls that shortly after her first child was born, Pat's second wife, Katharine, arrived at her doorstep with a full set of baby's clothes. She also says that Harry helped them buy their house. Some might argue that was the least they could do for the man who first got the idea to add cheese to the steaks.

Although others lay claim to making the first cheesesteak

Cooper, Al Martino, and the Three Stooges were other semiregulars. Maria Olivieri remembers more than one aspiring young entertainer "singing and dancing for soda" and the hope of running into someone famous. (Today some of those local kids who made it big gaze down on Pat's from a giant building mural—see page 21.)

In a city famously dead after dark, the sidewalk outside Pat's was teeming with excitement. No wonder the indoor sit-down restaurant that Pat opened right across Ninth Street in the mid-1950s flopped.

In 1964 Pat sold out his local business interests and retired to a ranch outside of Los Angeles with Evelyn and the kids. Although Pat's son, Herb, failed in both his 1980s attempts to franchise Pat's, the Ohio-based chains Steak Escape, Charley's Grilled Subs, Great Steak & Potato Company, and Penn Station were all successful nationally with the cheesesteak concept. The meat-processing companies Quality Foods and Gagliardi Brothers (the maker of Steak-umm) also helped to spread the cheesesteak's name and fame by marketing sliced and portioned steak sandwich meat that made it easier for people to serve and eat the sandwiches. In 1999 Quality celebrated the sale of its billionth cheesesteak by challenging Philadelphia residents to set a record for the most cheesesteaks eaten by a single city in a single hour (15,500 were consumed). Leading the charge was Mayor Ed Rendell (above), now the governor of Pennsylvania, whose love for the food, hefty build, and outgoing personality made him a worthy successor to Pat Olivieri in the role of cheesesteak ambassador.

The year 1999 was also marked by many cheesesteak product introductions: thirteen new cheesesteak foods hit the nation's supermarkets that year, or thirteen times the number introduced in 1997, according to market research company Mintel. And their popularity continues, judging from mid to late 2000s cheesesteak supermarket product introductions like Wal-Mart Philly Cheese Steak Sandwich Spread, Pringles Cheesesteak Potato Chips, and Philly Steak & Cheese Lean Pockets. This past decade also saw the cheesesteak debut on the menus of many national restaurants, thanks, in part, to the Amoroso Baking Company's new frozen roll division. For years people have said that it was not possible to make a good cheesesteak outside of Philadelphia because of Philadelphia's uniquely wonderful rolls, but the nationwide availability of Amoroso's rolls removed that argument.

In fact, this decade's introduction for limited time periods of Domino's cheesesteak pizza, McDonald's cheesesteak sandwiches, and Carl's Jr. cheesesteak burgers, and the more permanent addition of cheesesteaks to menus at Subway, Quiznos, Applebee's, Jack in the Box, and Johnny Rockets signaled the end of cheesesteaks as a regional specialty on the order of New Orleans's muffuletta and Miami's Cuban sandwiches and the beginning of their life as standard all-American fast food on a par with pizza, burgers, and the hot dogs Pat Olivieri invented the steak sandwich to escape.

PAT'S RINGSIDE SIDELIGHT

Say "boxing and Philly" and most everyone thinks Rocky. But Philadelphia also produced many real boxing stars, including International Boxing Hall of Famer Harold Johnson, managed for almost eight years by King of Steak crown-wearer Pat Olivieri.

Johnson was a great light heavyweight who had the misfortune of being a contemporary of great light heavyweight Archie Moore. Johnson turned pro in 1946 and won all twenty-four of his first fights before losing to Moore in 1949. Johnson lost to Moore in three of their next four matchups, including a 1954 championship challenge, before, as the Sunday *Philadelphia Bulletin* reported, Johnson "fell flat on his face" during a 1955 bout "without any noticeable assistance" from opponent Julio Medros. Johnson explained that he had eaten an orange that must have been poisoned in his dressing room before the fight.

Ostracized by almost everyone in the boxing establishment, Johnson succeeded in convincing fight fan and fellow Philadelphian Pat Olivieri to become his manager. After a string of wins and the National Boxing Association's decision to strip Moore of the lightweight championship for his failure to defend, Johnson captured the vacant title in a 1961 match against Jesse Bowdry. His 1962 win against Doug Jones was even more impressive. But even as Johnson was having his greatest success vanquishing opponents in the ring, Johnson was also battling his manager in court for $3,725, for not managing him correctly, and for taking friends and family to fights on Johnson's dime. "It is this last stab that sets Olivieri frothing like a milkshake machine," *Philadelphia Bulletin* sports columnist Sandy Gray wrote at the time. "I've spoiled him, the no-good." Oliveri told Grady before listing the cars, TV sets, movie cameras, drums, and expensive clothes Olivieri said he had bought "Prince Hal."

Nevertheless, Olivieri negotiated a new management contract somewhat more favorable to Johnson shortly after the Jones win. Olivieri was back as manager when Johnson lost his crown to Willie Pastrano on June 1, 1963.

In December 1963 Johnson told a newspaper reporter that he hadn't heard from Olivieri since his former manager's move to California, home to groves of (presumably untainted) oranges.

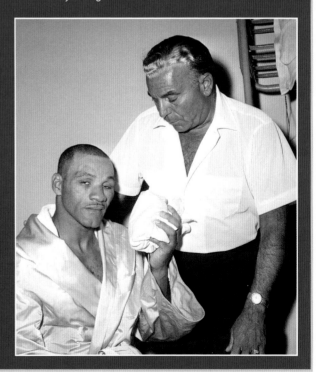

THE FAMOUS PHILLY MUSICIAN MURAL GAME

People waiting in line at Pat's can entertain themselves by singing the greatest hits of the aging rock 'n' roll stars on the mural across the street. With twenty-eight hundred murals and counting, Philadelphia has one of the largest mural arts programs of any city in the world. This four-story-high one, created in 2005, honors entertainers who grew up in the neighborhood. The musicians and singers are shown in framed portraits like the ones hanging on the walls of many local steak joints. For extra credit, see if you can find real photos featuring the same people on the walls at Pat's and Geno's (while one person in the party holds your place in line, of course.)

Answer key: The South Philly mural musicians and their greatest hits include Frankie Avalon ("Venus," "Why," "Dede Dinah"), Fabian ("Tiger," "Turn Me Loose," "Hound Dog Man"), Eddie Fisher ("Wish You Were Here," "Oh! My Pa-Pa," "Count Your Blessings"), Bobby Rydell ("Volare," "Kissin' Time," "Forgive Him"), Chubby Checker ("The Twist," "Pony Time"), and Al Martino ("Spanish Eyes," "I Love You Because").

CHAPTER 2:

HOMETOWN EATERIES

THE CHEESESTEAK IS CERTAINLY A GREAT-TASTING SANDWICH. BUT IN GREATER PHILADELPHIA, ITS REAL FLAVOR COMES FROM THE PEOPLE AND PLACES THAT SERVE IT. THE CLASSIC AND STILL-MOST-COMMON FORMAT IS AN OUTDOOR STAND, WHICH LENDS A BEACH-RESORT FEEL TO EVEN A MIDWINTER VISIT. BUT THAT'S CERTAINLY NOT THE ONLY TYPE OF EATERY ASSOCIATED WITH THIS SANDWICH. LOCAL CHEESESTEAK SPECIALISTS ALSO INCLUDE DELIS, PIZZERIAS, LUNCH COUNTERS, FAMILY RESTAURANTS, AND EVEN A BAR OR TWO.

DOES THIS CHAPTER PROFILE ALL THE PLACES THAT SERVE SUPERIOR CHEESESTEAKS IN GREATER PHILADELPHIA? DEFINITELY NOT. I HAVE TRIED TO INCLUDE THE MOST FAMOUS, POPULAR, AND HIGHLY REGARDED AS WELL AS THE OLDEST AND MOST INTERESTING. THEY ARE PRESENTED IN NONPARTISAN ALPHABETICAL ORDER WITH THE EXCEPTION OF PAT'S AND GENO'S, WHICH, BY VIRTUE OF THEIR LOCATION AT THE NINTH AND WHARTON BIRTHPLACE OF THE CHEESESTEAK AND THEIR POSITION AS THE LONGTIME EPICENTER OF CHEESESTEAK CULTURE AND COMPETITION, COME FIRST.

Pat's
King of Steaks

1237 PASSYUNK AVE., SOUTH PHILADELPHIA, 215-468-1546, WWW.PATSTEAKS.COM

Pat's was the first place to serve cheesesteaks. But is it the best? Just about all the local contests and food reviewers say no. Still, Pat's sells more cheesesteaks than any stand in Greater Philadelphia (with the possible exception of neighbor Geno's—neither stand will say exactly how many they sell). Joseph Groh of Chink's Steaks—no slouch in the cheesesteak-selling business himself—says he drove down Passyunk Avenue one Sunday afternoon recently and couldn't believe the line of tourists and cheesesteak pilgrims. Which is as it should be. Coming to Philadelphia in search of a cheesesteak and not going to Pat's is like going to the Holy Land and skipping Bethlehem. It's the originator that set the much-imitated standard for what a steak shop should feature: namely, an outdoor stand with separate food and drink windows, a Soup Nazi–style ordering system, and décor consisting of 8 x 10 glossy prints of celebrity tourists who have eaten here before.

Of the two steak shops located at what has been called the Fertile Crescent of cheesesteak culture, Pat's is the older and more demure. With its white clapboard siding, it looks a bit like a castle or a New England clam shack on steroids.

Pat's detractors say the staff is rude and its environs are not clean. Indeed, it's common to see french fries ground unceremoniously into the sidewalk plaque marking the spot where Sylvester Stallone filmed "the great motion picture *Rocky*" and vacationing CEOs looking as nervous as school

Frank Olivieri Jr.: He sure doesn't look rude to me.

kids at a spelling bee as they await their turn to order. But Frank Olivieri Sr., who took over the stand from his dad, Harry, and now works it with his son, Frank Jr., says both the trash and the ordering system are a consequence of the large scale of their business (see page 26)—and that people take the ordering rules on the "I. M. Hungry" sign too seriously. And how many times has anyone at Pat's actually suggested a patron follow step 4 ("if you make a mistake, go to the back of the line and start over")?

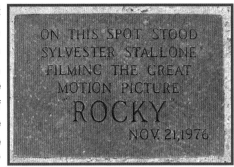

And if the critics are right and the cheesesteak you get is not the best, it is still your ticket to what is indisputably Philadelphia's best cheesesteak scene. The old men on the nearby row house stoops speaking Italian, the African American kids playing basketball in the court right across the street, and the stream of muscle cars, motorcycles, and limousines are a people-watcher's dream. If you're lucky you might even get to see a wedding party in full regalia: it's a longstanding tradition for Philly brides and grooms to sneak a cheesesteak between their wedding and the "formal" reception.

While it's true that most Philly neighborhoods have their own steak stand favorites (enough to fill a book, in fact), few keep Pat's 24/7 hours or are as convenient to the South Philadelphia sports stadiums. The stop at Pat's on the way to the game is a cherished ritual for local fathers and sons, as is the early-morning breakfast stop as a cap to a night of drinking. Some swear by the power of Pat's cheese, hot sauce, peppers, and steak to cure any hangover; others contend that you need to be drunk to really appreciate Pat's steaks.

TO GET THERE: From I-76 E, bear left onto I-676 E/Vine Street Expressway. Take the Eighth Street exit and turn right on Eighth. After about two miles, turn right on Reed Street. Take the first right onto Ninth Street. Pat's is located at the intersection of Ninth and Passyunk. By public transportation, take Bus 47 down Eighth until you see the buildings at Federal (walk one block west from Federal to Ninth, then one block south on Ninth).

SEATING: Outdoor tables

OFF-STREET PARKING: No

ALCOHOL: No

HOURS: 24/7

ROLL: Cut Liscio's loaf, except Sundays, when they use D'Ambrosio's

MEAT: Rib-eye, sliced at the shop; cooked ahead during busy periods (much of the time at Pat's)

ONION: Spanish white or yellow, diced and precooked

CHEESE: Whiz, provolone, American, or mozzarella, placed on the bread before the meat and onions

GRILL SEASONING: Soybean oil

POSSIBLY SCARY STORY: The ballpark adjacent to Pat's used to be a cemetery and the basement space that Pat's now uses to store soda was reportedly where an undertaker used to do his embalming.

RELATED LESS SCARY STORY: The tombstone supplier across from the cemetery made Pat's *Rocky* sidewalk plaque.

HOW TO ORDER:
A GUIDE FOR VISITORS

There is a protocol to ordering a cheesesteak at Ninth and Wharton, which, if not followed, can result in being sent to the back of the line Soup Nazi–style, or even worse, getting less meat. At Pat's and Geno's, you *must order* by saying the name of the cheese you want and then "with" or "without" (or as it is often pronounced in South Philly, "wit" or "witout"), which means with or without grilled onions. A correct and traditional order there would be "Whiz wit." "Mushrooms witout" will get you a steak sandwich with mushrooms but no onions or cheese. You order and pay for your drinks and fries at a separate window.

This ordering system is chiefly used at high-volume shops, which need to keep their lines moving quickly, or other places (many out-of-town) who cater to the tourist crowd and are trying to provide an "authentic" Philly cheesesteak experience. Although it's never a bad idea to step up to a restaurant ordering counter knowing what you want, slavishly adhering to the "wit or witout" phraseology at a more low-key neighborhood joint in Philly will mark you as a nervous tourist. Many of these out-of-the-limelight places don't even offer Cheez Whiz as an option. White American is the more common cheese default regionwide, along with provolone and sometimes mozzarella—both mild Italian cow's milk cheeses that melt easily. (Statistics in point: While a quarter of all Kraft's food service Cheez Whiz is sold locally, half of all its food service American cheese is sold here.) Keep in mind too that cooking the steak meat in whole slices, or "slab-style," is mainly a tradition in South Philly and the Northeast. In the rest of Philly and the world, the meat is usually finely chopped on the grill. Ask a place that normally prepares whole slices to chop the meat (or vice versa) per your personal preference with fear and trembling.

What is surprisingly acceptable, given the financial consequences, is to ask for your cheesesteak "inside out" or "gutted," or to ask your server to "scoop the roll." Any of these phrases will yield a cheesesteak with a higher meat-to-bread ratio and also leave the impression that you know what you are doing, always a good thing for a stranger in a strange town.

Pat's customers order in the shadow of celebrities who have come before.

FAMILY BEEFS

A visit to Pat's is a bonding experience and a fountain of fond memories for many families. But this same business has torn apart the Olivieri family that owns it.

The trouble started back in the late 1960s, when inventor Pat Olivieri decided to dissolve his interests. Lawyers hashed out an agreement that gave Pat's brother, Harry, the Ninth and Wharton stand and Pat's son, Herb, the Thirty-third Street one along with the rights to the Pat's name. But afterward Pat and Herb weren't speaking.

Harry and Herb weren't too friendly either, judging from the mid-1970s lawsuit Herb filed against the Ninth Street shop over signs it put up disassociating itself from some of Herb's franchises.

The next big Olivieri legal tussle followed Harry's retirement in the 1980s. In 1991 Harry's daughter, Maria, decided she wasn't getting her fair share of the business profits; the suits and countersuits and appeals between her and her brother, Frank, dragged on for several years. The upshot: brother and sister now only speak through lawyers, and, according to Maria, Frank did not attend their father's 2006 funeral.

Meanwhile, across town at the Reading Terminal Market, Herb and his son Rick were having problems of their own. One day in 1994, after decades working his dad's steak shops, Rick learned that he would not be getting Herb's Olivieri Prince of Steaks business. Rick quit, Olivieri's failed, and Rick opened his own Rick's Steaks in the same location. Once again, an Olivieri son didn't get what he expected. And once again, an Olivieri father and son were forever estranged.

In 2006 the third generation got into the act when Frank Olivieri Jr. sued his cousin Rick over the unlawful use of the Pat's crown logo and name at the Rick's stand.

In short, you can be sure that the Olivieris are not spending the two days of the year the Ninth Street stand is closed at a big happy holiday gathering of the extended family.

RIB-EYE RUMBLE

Say your family invents a food icon and sells it from a wildly successful stand, fending off parasitic competition like so many flies for forty years, and then a new guy opens up across the street and grows his business to the point where people hardly ever mention the name of your restaurant without naming his, almost as if you were in business together. You'd probably hate the guy's guts, right?

But Frank Olivieri Jr., grand-nephew of steak sandwich "king" Pat, and current proprietor of Pat's Steaks, says it's not true: "All that rivalry stuff is something the media invented. And he ran with it. His life's ambition seems to be to come up with these slogans like he's the 'Ace of Steaks.' And 'the Ace of Steaks beats the King.' We still generate ten times his trash, although probably a quarter of it comes from his place."

The unnamed "he," cross-street rival Joey Vento of the forty-year-old upstart Geno's, counters with indefinite pronouns of his own: "They used to clean once a day. Now they do more. They copied me, I didn't copy them." Still, he says it's useless. "They try to wet those sidewalks down and people are slipping and sliding all over the place, the grease is so embedded. To get it really clean, they'd have to rip the sidewalks up and start over."

Says Olivieri's father and business partner, Frank Sr., "All this clean, best of clean, it's because he's not doing the business." Olivieri Jr. chimes in, "As clean as he is, that's how busy we are."

Vento admits his lines are often shorter, but that's only because his operation is more efficient. He says, "In addition to the regular grill, I have a larger backup grill in back. If we get a big order, we cook it up back there so we don't have to hold up the line. It's my ace in the hole" (and possible inspiration for his 'Ace of Steaks' slogan?). "We don't have to pile meat up on the grill and serve it cold, like they do over there."

You get the idea. It's just like Olivieri Jr. said. There's no rivalry. No rivalry at all.

Geno's

1219 S. NINTH ST., SOUTH PHILADELPHIA, 215-389-0659, WWW.GENOSTEAKS.COM

Jimmy Vento in noncontroversial/grilling mode.

f Pat's is the Coney Island of steak shops, old and a bit worn but sure of its place in history and ability to please, then Geno's is Disney World, the younger, flashier upstart, offering its visitors what they're looking for and oh, so much more. Drive south on Tenth Street toward the two stands after dark, and Geno's building rises up from all the surrounding squat, dull row houses like Vegas in the desert. Visitors lured by the lights get a steak quite similar to the one served at Geno's older across-the-street rival but also get a chance to take a gander at owner Joe Vento's showroom of Harleys, study the brick walkway honoring police officers and firefighters killed in the line of duty, and look at the framed pictures of more (and more contemporary) celebrities than across the street.

Still, few of those stars are as colorful and interesting as Vento, the plain-talking, tattoo-wearing, motorcycle-riding sixth-grade expellee who became the right's unofficial national spokesman on immigration policy in late 2005 when he posted a sign reminding customers that it was America and asking them when ordering to "Speak English."

Geno's formerly Italian South Philadelphia environs has seen an increasing influx of Mexican and Asian immigrants in recent years. Vento has said the sign was born out of his frustration in trying to give these folks the steaks they want. Behind that frustration is Vento's own experience as the grandson of Italian immigrants who became a millionaire playing by the rules as they now stand. "These candidates keep

Geno's, pre-neon

Don't tell Al Gore but Geno's monthly electric bill is $5,000 ($8,000 if you include buildings across the street).

talking about how we need change," Vento says in the heat of the 2008 presidential primary race, the country song "Press One for English" blaring in the background. "Why? America is already great!" It certainly has been for him.

Joe Vento's father, James, opened Jimmy's Steaks, right across the street from Pat's and the current Geno's in the early 1940s (a place unrelated to the now-famous Jim's on Sixty-second Street and later on South). But James quickly got caught up in some less reputable business (see opposite page). When James Vento was jailed for murder in 1960, Joe left the army to help support the family. From the ordering window of his dad's business and (after Jimmy's went under) of another Ninth and Wharton steak shop named Joe's, Vento could see the building where his future steak shop would be. When the clothing and butcher stores in it closed, Vento got a $2,000 loan, two boxes of steak, some hot dogs, and a card-board Pepsi sign and opened Geno's. (He found the name graffitied on the building when he moved in.)

"I don't think I gave myself a salary for ten years," he says. Instead he put whatever money he made back into the business, especially into neon that, along with Vento's fanatical cleanliness, makes the place glow. "I love brightness," he says, stating the obvious. He also clearly loves the color orange and cops. In addition to having the "Path of Honor" memorializing fallen police officers and firefighters in front of his store and a police badge display case that runs along both sides of the building, Vento has held a number of fundraisers for the families of slain officers—a direct consequence of his family's shady ways. "In the old days if one family member was bad the whole family was supposed to be bad too," says Vento. "But I proved I was different. I've brought respect back to the Vento name."

TO GET THERE: From I-76 E, bear left onto I-676 E/Vine Street Expressway. Take the Eighth Street exit and turn right on Eighth. After about two miles, turn right on Reed Street. Take the first right onto Ninth Street. Geno's is located at the intersection of Ninth and Passyunk. By public transportation from Center City, take Bus 47 down Eighth and get off at Federal (when you see all the neon).

SEATING: Outdoor tables

OFF-STREET PARKING: No

ALCOHOL: No

HOURS: 24/7

ROLL: Liscio's roll

MEAT: Steer rib-eye, sliced by shop employees and pre-cooked and held in a warmer during busy times

ONION: Chopped and slightly precooked

CHEESE: Provolone, American, or Whiz (of which Vento is no fan)

GRILL SEASONING: Vegetable oil only

SPECIALTIES: Heart Attack Special, a steak featuring all three of the above cheeses

Among cops, anyway. Immigrants and those who sympathize with them sometimes give him the finger as they drive by; others won't eat there anymore. But Vento says they were far outnumbered by supporters in his legal battle with Philadelphia's Commission on Human Relations over the "Speak English" sign. (The agency ultimately ruled in his favor because Vento never refused service.)

Since then, some even more provocative items have appeared on Geno's window (a "Mexifornia" driver's license and a picture of a group of Iraqis being lynched among them). "Speak English," I suspect, is just one act in the ongoing political steak show that is Geno's.

HOW TO ORDER A CHEESESTEAK IN OTHER LANGUAGES

Think Geno's "speak English" policy is at worst discriminatory and at best, unfriendly? Make like a culinary Freedom Rider and order your cheesesteak with onions in another language: translations are below.

ITALIAN: Vorrei un panino con bistecca, cipolle grigliate e formaggio americano.

SPANISH: Quiero un "steak" de carne con cebollas y queso americano por favor.

MANDARIN CHINESE: Wo yao yi ge cheesesteak, jia yang chong he Cheez Whiz.

GERMAN: Ich möchte ein belegtes Steakbaguette mit Käse und Zwiebeln.

CZECH: Já bych cht?l jeden steak sendvi? s cibulí a americk?m s?rem.

FARSI: Beh man yek cheesesteak bah Cheez Whiz vah peeaz lotfan bedee.

PENNSYLVANIA DUTCH: Ich daed en Rinsfleesch uff Brot gleiche mit Zwiwwle un Cheese Whiz.

A VEGETARIAN ORDER IN MARATHI: Maala aak kanda aani paneer ghatalayla sandwich mans naaslayla dya.)

RUSSIAN: Mne pozhaluista buterbrod so steikom, s lukom i syrom.

THE VENTO CRIME FAMILY

Geno's owner Joey Vento grew up with a heritage of steaks and crime. And at the start of it all, the two were linked.

In fact, Joey Vento's father's criminal activity reportedly dates back to his beef with a man who told the Philadelphia health department that his Jimmy's Steaks stand was serving horsemeat. In 1960 James "Jimmy's Steaks" Vento was convicted of killing not that man but a hit man who had failed to carry out Jimmy's orders to kill this food critic.

If anything, Joey's brother, Steven "Steakie" Vento, was even more notorious. Between 1962 and 1986 Steven was arrested twenty-three times for crimes ranging from murdering his estranged wife's boyfriend and firebombing her house after she remarried, to counterfeiting, tax evasion, and a whole host of weapons and drug charges. Even after being convicted of drug charges and sent to prison in 1984, Steven continued to deal drugs, once bragging to a jury that he earned more than $1 million on one deal consummated behind bars.

But Steven's flashiest crime was a daring 1986 prison break scheme he planned with his son, Steven Jr., just months after Steven Jr. had been badly injured in a mob hit. The plan read like a Bruce Willis movie and called for a helicopter flown by a daredevil mercenary to land at Vento's maximum security prison, blast the guard towers with machine guns and a rocket launcher, and whisk Vento and a prisoner friend to freedom. But when the helicopter arrived at the prison at the appointed hour, it was piloted by tipped-off undercover law enforcement officers who merely hovered, leaving a puzzled Vento and his friend standing in the prison yard in their cranberry-juice-stained shirts (the sign that they were the prisoners to be airlifted).

Joey Vento has never been involved with any of this, and in fact tried to get his brother to go straight numerous times before Steven's 1991 death by heart attack. In other words, compared to the rest of his family, Joey is a downright angel.

THE CHEESESTEAK TEST

Some people blame the attacks on his war record from the Swift Boat Veterans for Truth; others, his statement during the first presidential debate that U.S. actions abroad should be subject to a "global test." But Philadelphians trace the beginning of the end of Senator John Kerry's hopes of capturing the presidency to the August 2003 day he showed up at Pat's King of Steaks and ordered a steak with Swiss cheese.

Swiss cheese, as any local knows, is not an option. But you might have thought Kerry had ordered Gruyère or blue for all the ridicule he received—not just from the local media but also in the *Washington Post* and on *Good Morning America* and BBC.

From time immemorial, the cheesesteak "triangle" at Ninth and Wharton has been the place for millionaire politicians like Kerry to prove they can get down and greasy with the commoners. One of Philadelphia's most successful politicians, former Philadelphia mayor and now Pennsylvania governor Ed Rendell, has eaten so many cheesesteaks in dress clothes that he has invented a variation of the "Philly lean" (see page 19) called "the Philly flip," in which you flip your tie over your shoulder to avoid grease stains. Kerry's advance people also might have taken a page from the campaign book of junk-food-loving Bill Clinton, who told the crowd at his Columbus Day 1992 Ninth and Wharton stop that the previous night's presidential debate with George Bush was "nothing tough, like whether Pat's or Geno's makes the best cheesesteaks," before buying food from both places.

Of course, that was well before Geno's "Speak English" sign went up. Since then, stopping at Geno's has been a way for politicians like Rick Santorum and Rudy Giuliani to establish their tough-on-immigration cred.

How important are cheesesteaks to Philadelphia voters? So important that on the day of Pennsylvania's hotly contested 2008 Democratic presidential primary, both candidates ate cheesesteaks: Hillary Clinton, a takeout chicken one from Boccella's restaurant in suburban Conshohocken, and Barack Obama, a rib-eye from Pat's. Anxious not to see history repeat itself, Michelle Obama ordered for her husband with a firm "Whiz with."

CELEBRITY WATCH

- Michael Bublé, the Backstreet Boys, and Nic Cage are all Geno's regulars. Britney Spears and Justin Timberlake used to be, although Geno Vento says the last two times Timberlake has come by with Pink, the crowds were so big they couldn't get off the bus.

- Boxer Joe Frazier has been spotted at Philip's, Larry's, and Pagano's.

- Overbrook native Will Smith called Overbrook Pizza's cheesesteaks the city's best on *60 Minutes*.

- Allen Iverson and Kobe Bryant have publicly praised Larry's.

- Actress Kim Delaney mentioned Dalessandro's on *Jay Leno*.

- Jimmy Buffett always gets a big order from Jim's whenever he's in town for a concert.

- In the WIP radio cheesesteak taste-off, chef Georges Perrier gave Chink's his highest rating.

- Singer Fabian says he used to eat up to five Pat's cheesesteaks at once after coming back from long stretches on the road.

- Actor Bruce Willis has called the cheesesteaks at the Roman Pantry in Carneys Point, New Jersey, the world's best.

Dear Mama – You look beautiful + we look good together! All my love, Tony Danza

Abner's

3813 CHESTNUT ST., WEST PHILADELPHIA,
215-662-0100, WWW.ABNERSCHEESESTEAKS.COM

Most basketball fans would cheer their team's 97-74 win. But when the whistle blew on the University of Pennsylvania Quakers' 23-point defeat of Florida Gulf Coast at the Palestra arena on November 18, 2006, the boos and hisses flew.

That's because nearby cheesesteak shop Abner's promises a free sandwich to all ticket holders whenever the Penn (or Drexel or St. Joe's) basketball team scores one hundred points at home, and the Quakers had come up three points short.

Penn fans have had their anticipatory chants of "cheesesteaks, cheesesteaks" answered four times in the past dozen years. In February 2002 Don Solomito's three-pointer with ten seconds left got the Quakers into the magical three digits, and 2,235 fans got free cheesesteaks. At about 1:30 a.m., Solomito showed up at Abner's to a hero's welcome (and to apologize to the staff).

"It's mayhem," says Abner's co-owner Stephen Mammino of those hundred-point nights. Fortunately, the Quakers only have competitors that bad about once every other year. Mammino also has the cheesesteak equivalent of the White House hotline—someone on the Penn sports department staff who will call Mammino on his cell when the score starts getting high. "I tell him to start yelling 'Defense,' and I check my supplies," Mammino says. Even on non-three-digit-scoring days, Palestra games so affect Abner's business that Mammino keeps as close tabs on college

Abner's Ivy League-ish dining room

sports schedules as he does on his payroll.

Abner's is also a frat boy favorite, which means Mammino always knows when it's pledge week. "The kids will come in here saying they need to get behind the grill and hug us or stand on a chair to get a picture of the Abner's

WARNING:

Five KFC chicken thighs contain 1,650 calories and 120 grams of fat. A Denny's Fabulous French Toast Platter will set you back 1,261 calories and 79 grams of fat. Or you could eat a twelve-inch Meat Lover's Pizza from Pizza Hut with its 2,960 calories and 176 grams of fat.

This is all to prepare you for and mellow you out about the 1,300 calories and 87 grams of fat in a cheesesteak. (And I am talking your average twelve-incher, not a Larry's Belly Filler.)

clock with their face in it," he says, shrugging. He declines to describe some of the things he's seen in four years of delivering to frat houses. At the time of this conversation Mammino was recovering from the Erin Express, a bus that takes college students from bar to bar the week of St. Patrick's Day and that had him fishing beer bottles out of Abner's toilets.

Abner's opened in 1983 as a solo business venture of South Street Jim's Steaks partner Abner Silver. (The "Since 1930" claim on Abner's menu board inaccurately refers to the Sixty-second Street Jim's, which actually opened in 1939.) A decade later Silver sold it to Gus Raptis, who Mammino joined in 2004. Echoes of Jim's deco design can be seen in Abner's aforementioned neon clock and the black-and-white tile floors. But Abner's is much bigger than either of those Jim's and has dark wooden tables like ones in an old college library. The walls are lined with articles about the free cheesesteak nights and framed photos of Penn and Drexel sports teams and somewhat obscure celebrities like Miss Coors, the Strawbs band, and former secretary of the treasury John Snow, who graciously agreed to sign his name under his printed signature on a dollar bill from the cash register.

TO GET THERE: Take the South Street exit off I-76 E. Turn right on South Street, which becomes Spruce Street. Turn right on Thirty-eighth Street, then turn left onto Walnut. Turn right on Thirty-ninth Street and then right on Chestnut. Abner's will be on the left near the end of the block. By public transportation, take the Market-Frankford subway line to the Fortieth Street stop, walk east two blocks to Thirty-eighth, turn right, and continue two blocks to Chestnut.

SEATING: For 80

OFF-STREET PARKING: Yes

ALCOHOL: Yes, beer

HOURS: 11 a.m. to midnight Sunday through Thursday, until 3 a.m. Friday and Saturday

ROLL: 9-inch Amoroso's roll

MEAT: Thinly sliced rib-eye

ONION: Chopped Spanish

CHEESE: Whiz-like cheese sauce, American, or provolone

GRILL SEASONING: Vegetable oil and oregano

SPECIALTIES: Signature coated waffle fries; house dressing used on chicken, salads, and hoagies

Big John's

1800 E. ROUTE 70, CHERRY HILL, NJ,
856-424-1186, WWW.BIGJOHNS.COM

What Pat Olivieri was to Philadelphia cheesesteaks, John Petzitello was to the same food in New Jersey: namely, a flashy, beloved figure who made a big success of his cheesesteak business.

Petzitello was physically big—about six feet tall—and so were his steak sandwiches. But the biggest things about Petzitello were his ideas: the free pickle bar featuring more than fifteen kinds of pickles, peppers, and relishes; the machine that made John's famous crinkle-cut french fries out of instant mashed potatoes; the pictures of other famous Johns (Kennedy, Wayne, Carson, Belushi, the Pope) that adorned the walls and the two "johns" (Olivia Newton- for the women's room, and Elton for the men's).

"When he did anything, he did it big," recalls Rose Marchese, who's waitressed at Big John's since 1979. "Like when he added the shakes, it was with all the different ice cream flavors—butter pecan, rocky road, and rum raisin—not just vanilla, strawberry, and chocolate."

Diners at this Big John's table are blessed by the cheesesteaks and the visage of Pope John Paul II.

A businessman who bought the Route 30 property as an extension of his real estate dealings, Petzitello opened Big John's in 1974 in a single building but soon bought up adjacent properties and expanded in size and offerings to include pizza (made by future Ishkabibble's owner Bart Brown) and a deli (run by Famous Deli family member Jerry Auspitz). Big John's even hosted a branch of Philly's Termini Bakery for a time. But the big seller and draw was always the cheesesteaks: the so-called mini cheesesteaks contained more than a third of a pound of meat; the "whole," more than a pound on twenty-two inches of bread.

Petzitello also had a big heart, according to former employees who remember the food he gave to charities and the day he closed the restaurant and bused all the help to Atlantic City to party. Gambling was the problem that led to his early 1990s bankruptcy, according to Sylvia Petalino, another former waitress. Petzitello died in 2004. But the restaurant still serves his huge cheesesteaks, signature french fries, and free pickles under pictures of famous Johns and continues to win best cheesesteak awards for Jersey.

TO GET THERE: From I-76 E, take the exit toward I-676 E and follow the signs for the Ben Franklin Bridge/US-30 E. Continue four miles on US-30 E, then take the right split for Marlton Pike/RT-70 E. After about five and a half miles, turn right at Marlkress Road, then left at Greentree Road. Turn left at Marlton Pike/RT-70 E. Big John's is located about a quarter of a mile down Marlton Pike/RT-70 E.

SEATING: For 199

OFF-STREET PARKING: Yes

ALCOHOL: No

HOURS: 11 a.m. to 8 or 9 p.m. daily

ROLL: 11-inch Del-Buono's for the half, two 11-inch Del-Buono's for the whole

MEAT: Chopped

ONION: Sliced and precooked into caramelized half-moon pieces

CHEESE: American, provolone, mozzarella, or Whiz (although American is most popular), all but the Whiz melted on the meat

GRILL SEASONING: None

SPECIALTIES: Crinkle-cut fries, pickle bar, ice cream shakes, and Big John's "special" steak with mushrooms, peppers, and sauce

Campo's

214 MARKET ST., OLD CITY, PHILADELPHIA
215-923-1000, WWW.CAMPOSDELI.COM

With its pert red, blue, and green awnings, polished maple window frames, and high-rent Old City location, Campo's seems too classy to serve a serious cheesesteak sandwich. It's an image that's reinforced inside by the brick walls, the counter help's Izod shirt "uniforms," and the real (rather than plastic) wicker sandwich baskets. But don't be fooled. Campo's began as a deli/butcher shop in Southwest Philly in the 1940s and only moved uptown in 2000 when that neighborhood started to go down. So they have both street and meat cred.

Co-owner Denise Campo (née Nanni) used to buy penny candy at the original Campo's at Sixty-second Street and Grays Avenue, after which the owner's son, Mike Campo, would sometimes gallantly walk her home. In 1975, with his parents' health failing, Mike and Denise became business partners at the store. One year later (much of which I assume was spent locked together in the storage room) they were married.

Mike and Denise added cheesesteaks to Ambrose and Rose Campo's original menu of deli sandwiches. "In the old store we used skirt steak," Denise admits. "But now we use rib-eye, fresh cut right here," she says, proudly holding up a card-sized bright red slice. That could explain why the shop now sells more cheesesteaks than anything else. The fact that it's one of only two freestanding steak shops in a historic area crawling with tourists hungry for an experience of this Philly specialty also probably helps.

Old City is also Philly's hipster restaurant and club headquarters. Despite this and its upscale—by cheesesteak standards—digs, Campo's maintains its family deli feel. Mike and Denise's kids, Michael and Mia, now work the chip-and-snack-cake-cluttered counter beside their parents and across from a painting of the original deli and a framed tribute to Tony "Tables," a recently deceased beloved elderly uncle who joshed with the customers while busing the tables.

TO GET THERE: From I-76 E, take I-676 E toward Central Philadelphia. Take the Benjamin Franklin Bridge exit, but instead of going on the bridge, stay on Sixth Street. After about half a mile, turn left on Market and go down four blocks. By public transportation, take the Market-Frankford subway line to the Second Street stop and walk half a block, or take the Regional Rail to Market East Station and walk eight blocks east down Market.

OTHER LOCATIONS: One cheesesteak stand (with a more limited menu) and several hoagie stands at the Wachovia Center

SEATING: 28 inside, 24 outside

OFF-STREET PARKING: No

ALCOHOL: Yes, beer

HOURS: 10 or 11 a.m. to 9 or 10 p.m. daily

ROLL: Liscio's loaf, cut to 9.5 inches

MEAT: Rib-eye, sliced on-site, served as slabs

ONION: Diced Vidalia

CHEESE: Whiz, white American, sharp provolone, hot jack, mozzarella, or almost anything else they have in-house, melted on the meat on the grill

GRILL SEASONING: Salt, pepper, and an olive and corn oil blend

SPECIALTIES: "I Got Mine at Campo's" T-shirts (a possible response to neighbor Sonny's "Bite Me" ones?), a mail order side business (see page 109), and Maggie Old-Fashioned Pizza Steak (made with fresh tomatoes instead of sauce)

Chick's Deli

906 TOWNSHIP LANE, CHERRY HILL, NJ
856-429-2022

You might think that the best Philadelphia cheesesteak would be made in—well, I don't know—maybe Philadelphia? So when *Philadelphia* magazine named Chick's Deli of Cherry Hill, New Jersey, Best Cheesesteak maker in their annual Best of Philly survey in 2003, the magazine got some well-deserved flack. In newspapers and on radio shows, editor Larry Platt attempted to defend its choice of not even some big, well-known Jersey steak shop but a back-alley deli whose sign doesn't even mention steaks.

In the magazine staff's blind taste test of fifteen steaks, including many from Philly, Chick's stood out for "beef, cheese, bread and grease [that] work together in perfect, almost feng shui-like unison, "the award write-up declared while acknowledging that it was likely "the first time cheesesteak and feng shui have ever been used in the same sentence."

Chick's co-owner Joe Danfield, who added cheesesteaks to the menu in 1984,

believes it's "the high-grade cut of meat we use" that wowed the magazine's editors (though he declines to name it) and the fact that the steak sandwiches are made fresh-to-order (like everything else).

In fact, the joint has been renowned locally as a source of both food and town gossip since Chick De Gregorio

Chick's Deli co-owners Joe Danfield (front) and Tony Della Monica

opened the doors in 1957. "When somebody who moved away comes back to town, the first place they come . . . is Chick's," Cherry Hill Fire Department Battalion Chief Mike Iannetta explained to a reporter at the time of the prize. Cherry Hillites seemed mainly surprised that the magazine was able to find Chick's. Its white bunker of a building on an alley off a street off Route 70 is so obscure and unimpressive that when Danfield brought his mother there just before he bought it in 1976, she burst into tears.

The August 2003 day *Philadelphia's* Best of Philly issue hit the stands was emotional in a different way. "All hell broke loose," notes Tony Della Monica, Danfield's normally quiet business partner. Ordering supplies in the quantities he and Danfield used to no longer met demand. "It was like the first week in business all over again," adds Danfield.

Things calmed down eventually, although to a level 15 to 20 percent higher than they were pre-award, including new, semi-regular phone calls from drivers on the Jersey Turnpike wanting directions.

TO GET THERE: From I-76 E, take the I-676 E toward Central Philadelphia. Take the Benjamin Franklin Bridge/US-30 E exit and follow the signs to cross the Benjamin Franklin Bridge. Continue on US-30 E and go about two miles, then bear left onto RT-38/Kaigns Avenue and drive half a mile. Bear right onto RT-70 E/Marlton Pike and drive on it for three miles, then turn left onto Edison Avenue/Georgia Avenue. Take the second right onto Pennsylvania Avenue, then the first right at Virginia. Turn right at Township Lane.

SEATING: 8 utilitarian tables in a windowless wing off the ordering area

OFF-STREET PARKING: Yes

ALCOHOL: No

HOURS: 7 a.m. to around 5 p.m. Monday through Saturday

ROLL: Liscio's loaf, halved

MEAT: Trade secret, but it is chopped fine on the grill—not because it's tough but because Danfield thinks it tastes better that way

ONION: Spanish onions, sliced into thin half-moons and rings, cooked fresh on the grill along with the meat for each sandwich, and eventually worked into the chopped meat

CHEESE: White American or provolone, melted on the meat on the grill. No Whiz—Danfield thinks it's too salty and drowns the taste of the meat.

GRILL SEASONING: Natural food juices only

Chink's

6030 TORRESDALE AVE., TORRESDALE, NORTHEAST PHILADELPHIA, 215-535-9405

Chink's Steaks is time travel on an Italian roll, from its hand-jerked soda fountain to its wooden booths and tin ceilings to its racial slur of a name. It's also one of the most highly praised steakeries in the city, its sandwiches ranking second only to John's Roast Pork in recent contests and critic surveys.

Chink's founder and namesake was a white Jewish man named Samuel Sherman who acquired his un-PC moniker as a seven-year-old schoolboy with almond-shaped eyes. After working at the Thirty-third Street Pat's

would be here and his wife, Milly, would be there," Groh says, pointing to stairs going to the second floor in the back of the shop, "and start yelling at him and he'd shout back, no matter who was in here."

Chink was also "quite a salesman," in a way that some found hard to take. "He would say, 'Hey, why don't you have a black and white [shake]?' And before you'd know it, you'd have one, even if you didn't want it. There was no liking Chink—you either loved him or hated him," says Groh, obviously among the former.

"There was no liking Chink— you either loved him or hated him."

Steaks and for the military in Washington State during World War II, Sherman opened a steak shop in an old soda fountain/candy store right across the street from a movie theater. But current owner Joseph Groh says the show inside the shop was sometimes just as good. "He'd come in after a night of gambling, all tired and grumpy. Chink

Groh first knew Chink as the man in the window grill on his paper route. At sixteen, Groh got an after-school job peeling onions and cleaning the floors at Chink's. Now Groh's the guy in the window making the steaks just the way Chink did, although it seems as if Groh's steaks are even more widely known and praised. "I might be putting a

little more meat than Chink did, especially if he had lost money [gambling] the night before," Groh explains.

Groh also employs teenagers, mainly girls who are as sweet as the sundaes, egg creams, and malteds they make. Groh says old-fashioned drinks and methods can require explanation with younger customers, like the woman who complained about her banana milk shake's strong taste because she had never had one made with real banana.

By contrast, awareness and sensitivity to racial issues has increased so much since the late 1940s that in 2004 a woman launched a campaign to get Groh to change the shop's name. While Groh thus far seems about as likely to do that as he is to get rid of his malteds, a second shop he opened in South Philly in mid-2008 simply adopted the name of the former restaurant on that site—Tugboat Annie's.

TO GET THERE: Take I-95 N to the Harbison exit. Keep right at the fork to continue toward Aramingo Avenue. Merge onto Aramingo Avenue, which becomes Harbison. After about three-quarters of a mile, turn right at Torresdale. Chink's is on the left, about half a mile down Torresdale. By public transportation, take the Market-Frankford subway line to the Erie/Torresdale stop and take Bus 56 to Torresdale Avenue and Comly Street. Walk a block northeast on Torresdale Avenue.

OTHER LOCATIONS: Tugboat Annie's, 901 S. Columbus Blvd., 215-271-5940 (takeout only)

SEATING: Fountain stools and booths for about 30

OFF-STREET PARKING: No

ALCOHOL: No

HOURS: 10 or 11 a.m. to 7 or 8 p.m. Monday through Saturday

ROLL: Cut Liscio's loaf or 10-inch roll, warmed on the grill

MEAT: Rib-eye, thinly sliced on-premises, broken but not chopped

ONION: Cooked with the meat

CHEESE: American or provolone (no Whiz)

GRILL SEASONING: A little Wesson

SPECIALTIES: Hand-pumped cherry and vanilla Cokes, egg creams, shakes, and malteds

Samuel Sherman shortly after he opened his shop

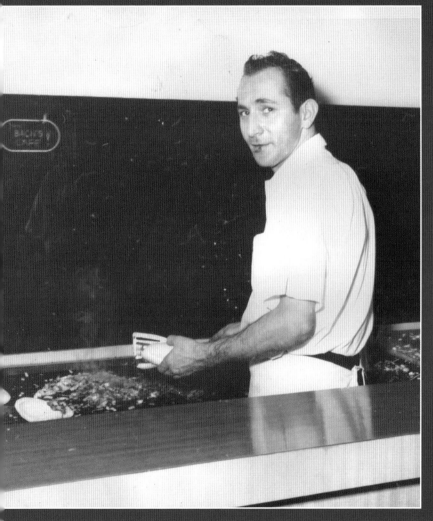

Joseph Groh at the grill

Chubby's

5826 HENRY AVE., ROXBOROUGH, PHILADELPHIA

215-487-2575

Pat's and Geno's may be the most famous cross-street cheesesteak rivalry in Philadelphia, but another almost-as-heated cheesesteak battle has been going on in Roxborough for more than twenty years. Dalessandro's is the Pat's of Henry Avenue in being older and somewhat better known; Chubby's is the Geno's-style challenger-leech. Both feature limited indoor seating, beer, and near-identical framed posters of peppers and/or onions, and both serve their chopped steak sandwiches stabbed with forks in cheery red plastic wicker baskets.

But where Dalessandro's is a luncheonette that serves beer, Chubby's is a diner-turned-bar—a transformation aided by the mountain of liquor signs and bottles that now faces the former lunch counter. All forty-plus offerings in Chubby's impressive beer selection come in frosted mugs. Also unlike Dalessandro's, Chubby's has a small parking lot and is open on Sundays—a competitive advantage owner Rich Phelps advertises out front on a Rent-a-Sign. The shop's main sign pictures Chubby's founders, two skinny guys of opposite heights, one of whom reportedly trained with Pudge Carbone of Pudge's—hence the fatty name.

Rich Phelps used to be a lot Chubbier.

TO GET THERE: Take I-76 W to the 340A/Lincoln Drive exit. Bear right, following the signs for Ridge Avenue West, and follow Ridge about one and a half miles to Walnut Lane. Turn right on Walnut and drive two blocks to Henry. Turn left. Chubby's will be one block up on the left. Public transportation options include Bus 32 or Bus 65 (down Walnut Lane to Henry) or Bus 23 (down Henry to Wendover).

SEATING: 5 booths plus the lunch counter

OFF-STREET PARKING: A small lot

ALCOHOL: Yes

HOURS: 11 a.m. to 1 or 2 a.m. Monday through Saturday, until 11 p.m. Sunday

ROLL: Amoroso's, with both ends intact

MEAT: Rib-eye, sliced and finely chopped

ONION: Spanish, cut in 1.5-inch squares for maximum taste impact, cooked in batches several times a day

CHEESE: Whiz; or American, provolone, or Swiss, melted on the grill

GRILL SEASONING: Just enough fat to get the grill started

SPECIALTIES: Beer, homemade hot peppers, and cheesesteak on lettuce—a low-carb option that owner Rich Phelps partly credits for helping him drop seventy pounds, thus ending the common assumption that the shop was named after him.

Claymont Steak Shop

3526 PHILADELPHIA PIKE, CLAYMONT, DE
302-798-0013

Most serious steak shops slice their own rib-eye. But the Claymont Steak Shop may be the only Philly area shop that doubles as a wholesale meat operation. So Claymont not only slices rib-eye for its own sandwiches but also does it for other shops and even retail customers. Pick up a five-pound box of its meat, a couple of dozen rolls, and some cheese, and go home and pretend you are Pat Olivieri.

This makes Claymont sound big, and it is. Three places the size of Steve's Prince of Steaks on Roosevelt Boulevard would fit in the restaurant part alone, which includes separate areas to order, pick up, and eat in. The open kitchen, where twelve to fifteen people scurry, is almost as big again. The self-service tables in the center can seat almost one hundred; that, plus the parking lot and the shop's location right off I-495, would make it seem like

Demi Kollias with her two daughters, Kelly, 12 (left) and Georgia, 10

Pick up a five-pound box of Claymont's meat, a couple of dozen rolls, and some cheese, and go home and pretend you are Pat Olivieri.

a bus driver's dream and, it usually follows, a food lover's nightmare.

But Claymont is an exception, judging from the number of local newspaper best cheesesteak awards lining the walls and the number of locals who come here often enough for thirty-nine-year-old owner Demi Kollias to recognize and greet by name.

Among a very elite group of steak shop owners holding an MBA, Kollias already owned several 7-Elevens when she approached her uncle, Bob Hionis, about buying his forty-year-old restaurant and wholesale steak business. Still, he was skeptical; in fact, Kollias says, "He told me that in six months I would be begging for him to take it back." Not only has that not happened, but the petite Greek native has actually increased the demands of the business by adding new delivery and catering services. "When we're busy it's exciting. It's like you're flying," she says, sounding like someone high on Cheez Whiz.

TO GET THERE: From I-95 S, take exit 11 toward Port of Wilmington/Baltimore and merge onto I-495 S/Vietnam Veterans Memorial Highway. After about a mile, take the Claymont exit onto US-13/Philadelphia Pike. Claymont Steak Shop is located about half a mile down the Philadelphia Pike on the left.

SEATING: For almost 100

OFF-STREET PARKING: Yes

ALCOHOL: No

HOURS: 10 or 11 a.m. to 11 p.m. or midnight Monday through Saturday, 11 a.m. to 9 p.m. Sunday

ROLL: Rolls handmade for the shop by Wilmington's M & M and Serpe and Sons bakeries "so the size isn't always the same," cut on the top instead of the side so the generous portion of meat stays in

MEAT: Australian rib-eye, sliced on-premises so thinly that little chopping is required (although the presentation is chopped)

ONION: Cut into quarter slices, precooked, and thoroughly blended with the meat and cheese

CHEESE: Default is American, but provolone, mozzarella, or Whiz are available on request

GRILL SEASONING: Water, used only when they're busy and want to speed up the cooking

SPECIALTIES: Steak fries, cheesesteak pizza, and cheesesteak salad

Cosmi's Deli

1501 S. EIGHTH ST., SOUTH PHILADELPHIA
215-468-6093, WWW.COSMIDELI.COM

When life gives you lemons, make lemonade, is the time-honored antidote for bad luck. When a fire caused extensive damage to Cosmi's Deli in July 2000, the Seccia family did the Philadelphia equivalent: they made cheesesteaks on the grill they added during the shop's nine-month restoration. This not only boosted business but also resulted in their little white corner deli being declared "the real king of steaks" by *Philadelphia* magazine after a 2004 taste test of their cheesesteak and forty-nine competitors.

That was only the most recent transformation of this seventy-five-year-old family business. Cosmi's opened in 1932 as a combination butcher shop and grocery—the Acme of its day. Cans and boxes were stacked to the ceiling, and picture windows showcased shop-cured hams and meat from former family pets.

Founder Cosmi Quaddrone was very religious and so devoted to Saint Francis, his animal lover patron saint, that he refused to eat his own meats on Wednesdays or Fridays, Cosmi's now sixty-six-year-old nephew, Leon Seccia, recalls. He could also be "crafty," deliberately leaving money out in the store as a test of employee honesty.

With the rise of supermarkets and busy two-career families in the 1960s and 1970s, takeout hoagies became the focus of business and acclaim until the fire and *Philadelphia* magazine rebirth of 2004, when cheesesteaks became the shop's best seller. In addition to the publicity from that award and its 2008 replay, Leon's son, Mike, attributes their steaks' popularity to meat from the Original Philadelphia Cheesesteak Company (see page 82) and personal service that only a small business can provide. People who want to share a sandwich can get different toppings on the different halves, and at least once, tourists who had trouble following Mike's directions got a personal escort to a nearby water ice stand. And while Cosmi's is not yet as popular or famous as the nearby cheesesteak assembly lines, Mike is showing definite signs of Joey Vento/Tony Luke–like marketing acumen in naming sandwiches after local celebrities and in his catering operation's unique make-your-own, all-you-can-eat cheesesteak bar.

Cosmi's founder Cosmi Quaddrone mans the meat counter with his wife Pauline in the late 1940s. In front is nephew and future owner Leon Seccia, 4.

TO GET THERE: From I-76 E, bear left onto I-676 E/Vine Street Expressway. After about a mile and a half, take the Eighth Street exit and turn right on Eighth. Go about two miles down Eighth. Cosmi's Deli is to the left, at the intersection of Eighth and Dickinson. By public transportation, take Bus 47 to Eighth and Dickinson.

SEATING: Only the front stoop and a couple of plastic tables and chairs on the sidewalk in the summer.

OFF-STREET PARKING: No

ALCOHOL: No

HOURS: 10 a.m. to 9 p.m. Monday through Saturday, 11 a.m. to 7 p.m. Sunday

ROLL: Your choice of Aversa's or the harder, seeded Sarcone's

MEAT: Marinated blend of loin tail and rib lifter meat from the Original Philadelphia Cheesesteak Company known as WOW

ONION: A small amount, diced and mixed in with the cooking meat

CHEESE: All the usual choices, melted on the meat on the grill

GRILL SEASONING: None (although Wow has its own seasoning)

SPECIALTIES: Chicken cheesesteaks made from boneless, skinless breast meat; a vegetarian primavera sandwich with grilled vegetables; and the self-serve cheesesteak "bar," featuring hot chafing dishes of meat, rolls, chicken, sauce, onions, cheese, and peppers (for groups and parties)

THE STAFF OF THE STEAK
(OR JUST ANOTHER INGREDIENT?)

The bread makes the steak. You can't get bread this good anywhere else in the world. It's because of the water in Philly, a common explanation goes.

But this is not an explanation commonly made by Philadelphia breadmakers. On the contrary. "It's not about the water or even the formula," says Leonard Amoroso Jr., executive vice president of Philadelphia's largest and best-known steak roll maker. "It's about process—how long you mix the doughs, what temperature your doughs are at, all that stuff." Chad Vilotti, vice president of Amoroso rival Liscio's, thinks the great local demand from steak shops "who want these type of rolls delivered fresh every day" is also part of the reason.

Early neighborhood bakeries delivered door-to-door as well as to corner mom-and-pop stores and, later, to the steak stands that also started in South Philly. If a steak stand ran out of bread, the owner could just run down the street for more. If the quality of one baker's rolls started to slip, it was easy to find another. (In fact, by the early 1940s, Vilotti says, most of the rolls were being delivered by independent distributors who, rather than go to the trouble of talking to a baker about a problem a steak shop customer was having with his product, would just switch the account to another of their many client bakeries, sometimes without even telling the customer.)

But like other businesses, the steak bread one has consolidated in recent years. Many of the small family bakeries in South Philly have closed or been bought up and seen their business going to bigger bakeries like the old and well-known Amoroso's and the newer and rapidly growing Liscio's.

Philly cheesesteak rolls can be soft, hard-crusted, or somewhere in between. The hard-crusted rolls are represented by small South Philly bakeries like Sarcone's and Carangi's. These rolls are favored by stands that make juice-filled cheesesteaks and roast pork sandwiches because they will stand up to a wet sandwich (but are called gum-bleeders by deriders or mistaken as stale by tourists). On the other end of the hardness scale, and more acceptable to many more people, are Amoroso's and Del-Buono's, with their soft interiors and extremely

pliable crust. The hoagie rolls made by the late Vilotti-Pisanelli Bakery for many years were, by all reports, somewhere between these two extremes, and these were the rolls of choice for some of the highest-profile shops in town, including Pat's, Geno's, and John's Roast Pork, up until the early 2000s, when customers say the rolls began suffering from "inconsistency problems." That's steak shop talk for "never the same size."

Enter Liscio's, a Glassboro, New Jersey, bakery co-owned by the Vilotti bakery founder's great-grandson, Chad Vilotti, which had, according to Chad, "developed a roll very similar to the old Vilotti's." Defections from Vilotti-Pisanelli to Liscio's by Pat's and Geno's and other steak shops helped Liscio's grow an amazing 100 percent between 2004 and 2006. Meanwhile, the still larger Amoroso's is seeing some of its strongest growth from rolls that they flash-freeze and ship to shops interested in recreating "authentic" Philly cheesesteaks at restaurants around the country.

ROLL CALL: A RUNDOWN OF WHO'S BUYING FROM WHAT LOCAL BAKERY.
(NOTE: A few stands use more than one supplier.)

AMOROSO'S: Abner's, Chubby's, Dalessandro's, Jim's, Larry's, Pagano's, Sonny's, Talk of the Town

AVERSA'S: Cosmi's Deli

CARANGI: Dakota Pizza, John's House of Pork

CONSHOHOCKEN: Pepperpot, Pudge's, John's Pizza

D'AMBROSIO'S: George's, Gooey Louie's, Pat's (Sundays only)

DEL-BUONO'S: Big John's, Donkey's

DEPALMA'S: Grey Lodge Pub

LISCIO'S: Campo's, Chick's Deli, Chink's, Geno's, Johnny's Hots, Pat's, Rick's Steaks, Shank's & Evelyn's, Spataro's, Steaks on South, Tony Luke's

SARCONE'S: Cosmi's Deli, George's

Dakota Pizza Company

333 E. LANCASTER AVE., WYNNEWOOD, PA
610-642-6770, WWW.DAKOTAPIZZA.COM

Healthy, low-fat, and gourmet are not words typically associated with cheesesteak purveyors. But they're all over the menu of Dakota Pizza Company, along with the slogan "Not Your Typical Pizza Shop."

I'll say. Stephen Bledsoe is a culinary school grad who spent most of his career at fine-dining spots Passerelle, Bravo Bistro, and Big River Fish Company. And he says his intent in opening the Dakota Pizza Company in a little Wynnewood strip mall in 1999 was to "apply those same skills to everyday food." Given his location just a parking lot away from a Whole Foods in Philadelphia's affluent suburban Main Line and just a few miles from Haverford and Bryn Mawr colleges, making the food as healthy as possible was another no-brainer.

Which brings us to his cheesesteaks. "We're not necessarily saying they're healthy," says Bledsoe. "But we make them as good as they can be." That means using "lean" top round, as does Jim's, one of Bledsoe's favorite Philly steak spots, instead of the fattier rib-eye. Bledsoe sautés the beef with a 10 percent olive oil, 90 percent vegetable oil blend, then combines it with chopped onions that have been pre-cooked with kosher salt, dried thyme, and a pinch of sugar. Then he trowels the whole thing into Carangi seeded rolls, like those used at Bledsoe's other favorite Philly cheesesteak joint, John's Roast Pork. The result, Bledsoe boasts, "is as good as any steak you'll find in Philly, and on a better roll

than used by many. Blindfolded, you'd probably think it was from South Philly."

In 2004 *Philadelphia* magazine agreed, giving Dakota's cheesesteak 4.5 out of a possible 5 "clogged arteries" in a fifty-cheesesteak survey, a score second only to that of winner Cosmi's Deli (see page 50).

Stephen Bledsoe showing off his "gourmet" cheesesteak

TO GET THERE: From I-76 W, take exit 13 to St. David's/Villanova onto Lancaster Avenue (US-30). Dakota Pizza Company is located five and a half miles down Lancaster, on the left. By public transportation, take Regional Rail R5 to Wynnewood Station. From there, walk southwest on East Wynnewood Road, then right onto Lancaster for about a tenth of a mile.

SEATING: For 35 in a casual, deli-style setting

OFF-STREET PARKING: Yes

ALCOHOL: No

HOURS: 11 a.m. or noon to 8 or 10 p.m. daily

ROLL: Carangi seeded loaf, cut to 11.5 inches

MEAT: Top round, thinly sliced and chopped

ONION: Chopped and precooked on the grill with oil, salt, sugar, and thyme (almost to the point of caramelization)

CHEESE: American, provolone, Cheez Whiz, or mozzarella

SEASONING: Vegetable and olive oil blend

SPECIALTIES: Roasted red pepper steak topping option, homemade soups and meatballs, popular chunk-style chicken cheesesteaks

STORY BEHIND THE NAME: "I wanted something that sounded American, and *Dakota* is a Native American word. I didn't want to call it Tony's or Luigi's," says Bledsoe (although he is half-Italian and has never been to either of the Dakotas).

Recommended Liquid Accompaniments

SOFT DRINKS: Traditional favorites are birch beer and Wishniak cherry soda. Birch beer is a Northeastern favorite, similar to root beer in age and origin but made with birch bark (really!) instead of sarsaparilla root, which gives it more of a wintergreen kick. Wishniak is a type of dark cherry grown in Eastern Europe familiar to Jewish-owned Philadelphia bottlers of old like Frank's.

BEER: Where you can get them, try local India pale ales like Flying Fish HopFish, Victory HopDevil, or Philadelphia Brewing Company's Newbold IPA. And you can't go wrong with a lager from America's oldest brewery, the 180-year-old Pennsylvania-based Yuengling (*ying-ling*). Don't worry if you forget the weird name: order a lager anywhere else in America and you'll get a Bud; in Philly you'll get a Yuengling and it's *much* more interesting.

WINE: Choices include a red Zinfandel, Cabernet Sauvignon, Chianti, or Merlot. In other words, there is no consensus among the few who like to drink wine with their cheesesteaks other than it should be red.

Dalessandro's

600 WENDOVER ST., ROXBOROUGH, PHILADELPHIA, 215-482-5407

Dalessandro's is on the short list of virtually every serious cheesesteak connoisseur in the city. The reason, family member Fran Dalessandro Sack believes, is simply that "we use good quality food and we give people a good amount of it for their money."

The meat is rib-eye, sliced fresh in the building's basement, chopped fine, and placed on Amoroso's hoagie rolls along with the onions—especially the onions. They are also hand-sliced, then sautéed in an olive and vegetable oil blend another door (à la gas station).

This tiny former grocery store is reportedly actually an improvement on the Ridge and Manayunk location where Sack's father, William Dalessandro, a student of local street food, first decided to perfect the steak sandwich in 1960. He thought big, wide Henry Street would bring in more business. Fran's mother, Betty, took over after William got sick in the late 1980s. Fran and her brother, Tom, took over when she died—Fran, with reluctance. So when her brother died in late

"When I told people that I had sold, I thought they were going to cry."

and left to simmer on the grill in a mound until a "steak wit'"is ordered. "Everyone loves the onions." Sack says. "One woman used to come in and tell us to just put a tiny bit of meat and fill the rest of the roll with onions."

Certainly people don't patronize Dalessandro's for the atmosphere, which is a cross between a school cafeteria and a soup kitchen. Folding chairs line the shop's two big plate-glass window walls, facing in so as to offer the best possible view of the butts of the people eating at the small counter. The décor is basement rec room circa 1963, and anyone needing the rest room has to go outside and enter through

HAVE YOU HEARD THE GOOD NEWS?

DALESSANDRO'S
STEAK & HOAGIE SHOP
OPENS TODAY AT
(THURSDAY, SEPT. 26)
HENRY AVE. & WALNUT LANE
(FORMERLY AT   (HENRY AVE. And
RIDGE & MANAYUNK AVES.)   WENDOVER ST.)

TRY OUR DELICIOUS SPECIALS

- CHEESE STEAKS   · PEPPER STEAKS
- MUSHROOM STEAKS   · MEATBALL SANDWICHES
- SAUSAGE SANDWICHES   · AND OUR SPECIALTY:
                                          ITALIAN
Milk Shakes And All Cold Beverages Can Be   HOAGIES
Included With Your Sandwich Order For Delivery

OPENING HOURS:
11 A.M. to 1 A.M.
DAILY
11 A.M. TO 2 A.M.
Friday & Saturday
Continuing Our
DELIVERY SERVICE
IV 2-5407
IV 2-5416

2007, she started looking for a buyer. "When I told people that I had sold, I thought they were going to cry," she says. Meaning longtime employees? "No, customers!"

Sack continues to be amazed by the intensity of customer feeling about the shop. She recalls, "There would be people who would come in here and say, 'We just landed at the airport.' They would come here before checking into their hotel. Then they'd come every day they were in town."

And when the shop would close Easter week for its annual spring cleaning, she says, "I would be standing on the grill with a rag in my hand and people would still bang on the door, begging us to make them a sandwich."

New owner Alexandro Apsis has already gotten a taste of Dalessandro's fans' fanaticism. One woman walked in, heard news of the sale, and then walked out again, vowing never to return. A lot of people have told him not to change anything. "What do they mean by that?" Apsis asks. "Do they mean the food? Do they mean the place? Because there are holes in the tile on the floor, and the Formica counter is peeling and other things the health inspectors don't like."

The son of a butcher who went on to own the popular Explorer's Den and Pagano's steak shops, Apsis says, "I know what I'm doing. If I change anything, it will only be to make it better."

THE STORY BEHIND THE FORKS

Fran Dalessandro Sack thinks the custom of stabbing steaks with plastic forks started when customers began using the spoons Dalessandro's had for coffee to eat the pieces of chopped meat that overflowed into the sandwich baskets. Somehow it evolved into a fork that is now standard service at virtually all Roxborough/Manayunk area steak shops—and almost nowhere else.

TO GET THERE: Take I-76 W to the 340A/Lincoln Drive exit. Bear right, following the signs for Ridge Avenue West, and follow Ridge about one and a half miles to Walnut Lane. Turn right on Walnut and drive three blocks to Magadelena. Take the first left onto Wendover. Dalessandro's is located toward the end of the block, to the right. Public transportation options include Bus 32 or 65 (down Walnut Lane to Henry) or Bus 23 (down Henry to Wendover).

SEATING: For about 30 on the aforementioned folding chairs and stools

OFF-STREET PARKING: No

ALCOHOL: Beer only

HOURS: 11 a.m. to midnight Monday through Saturday

ROLL: Amoroso's

MEAT: Rib-eye, sliced in house and chopped fine

ONION: Chopped and precooked

CHEESE: No Whiz for years, but new owner Apsis has added it. Everything else is melted on the meat as it's cooking and placed cheese side down on the roll, so it can be hard to see.

GRILL SEASONING: Oil and water

Donkey's Place

1223 HADDON AVE., CAMDEN, NJ,
856-966-2616

Camden, New Jersey, has been called America's most dangerous city. Driving down Haddon Avenue in the Pollocktown section of the city on crumbling asphalt through block upon block of bombed-out buildings, that moniker is easy to believe. That is, until you get to the bustling, well-kept yellow-brick Donkey's Place, a sterling example of the staying power of a really good sandwich.

Open the corner door and you'll find a museum of the days before the shipyard and the Campbell's and RCA factories closed, taking their jobs with them. The beautiful dark wooden bar is surrounded by old-fashioned soda machines, a Budweiser-Clydesdale lamp, framed pictures of athletes from the early 1900s, and two pianos from the days when Donkey's hosted live music in the evenings. But probably the most lasting memory people have of this place—their unique cheesesteaks—still sizzle away on the grill at the end of the bar.

The steaks were never made with donkey meat, bar owner Robert Lucas reassures. Donkey was just the nickname his dad, light heavyweight championship boxer Leon Lucas, acquired because people said he had a punch like the kick of a mule. In 1943, with his boxing career largely over, Leon Lucas bought the bar, which still has the remnants of the bell warning system from its speakeasy days.

Robert Lucas isn't exactly sure when or how his dad got the idea for the Donkey cheesesteak, with its signature folded-over slice of rib-eye, round super-poppy-seeded kaiser roll, and whole stack of curly, caramelized onions. "He certainly had been to Pat's in Philadelphia. There was a Polish bakery that sold kaiser rolls right up the street. And being Polish, he ate a lot of onions," Lucas said, while sipping an O'Doul's.

Robert Lucas with his dad's creation

DONKEY

Indeed, onions are the dominant taste of a Donkey's cheesesteak. Anyone who eats one better like them and hang with people who also do. The roll's extra blast of poppy seeds has also been a concern in recent years of customers on probation for its effect on their urine tests. Despite this, Lucas sells four hundred sandwiches on a good day to neighbors and employees of the nearby medical centers.

As you leave you may notice the axe from "the last Market Street ferry" that hangs ominously over the door—although Lucas insists there is no Rube Goldberg–style string attached to catch bill skippers.

Pictures of Donkey in his 1920s' fighting heyday hang above the bar.

TO GET THERE: From I-76 E, take the exit for I-676 E/Ben Franklin Bridge/US-30 E. Turn right at Sixth Street and merge onto Benjamin Franklin Bridge/US-30 E. After crossing the bridge, take the left fork onto US-30 E/Admiral Wilson Boulevard toward New Jersey Turnpike/Cherry Hill/Trenton and go one and a half miles. Take the Baird Boulevard South exit and merge onto Baird Boulevard/CR-608. After about half a mile, bear right onto Kaighns Avenue. Take the second left onto Haddon. Donkey's Place will be on the right.

OTHER LOCATIONS: Donkey's Too, 7 Tomlinson Mill Rd., Medford, NJ, run by Lucas's kids; and a Donkey's Place franchise in Ocean City (see page 142).

SEATING: 12 bar stools and several small tables

OFF-STREET PARKING: A very small lot adjacent to the building

ALCOHOL: Yes

HOURS: 10 a.m. to 6 p.m. Monday through Friday

ROLL: Custom-made kaiser—larger and with extra seeds—from Del-Buono's Bakery of Haddon Heights, New Jersey

MEAT: Rib-eye, folded

ONION: Slices, slow-cooked in a corner of the grill to a saucy goo

CHEESE: White American only

GRILL SEASONING: None, but Lucas's dad's secret seasoning (paprika, definitely; garlic, sesame, possibly), goes on the onions or meat

EATING RECORD: Several people have eaten six steaks in a single seating, but only one guy ate six steaks washed down with six bottles of beer. "He wasn't even heavyset. He was a skinny guy who claimed to be going home to have dinner with his wife," recalls the still-visibly-astonished Lucas.

LA·DI·DA CHEESESTEAK

They might have been spurred by the Wyndham's late 1990s Gourmet Cheesesteak Contest (see page 148) or by rich people who want a taste of how the other half eats (but not if it means waiting in line at Pat's). Whatever the cause, gourmet riffs on Philly's favorite sandwich have become a point of pride (and fun) for chefs at high-end restaurants throughout Greater Philadelphia. Here are a few of the most visible recent examples. (Check out the recipe chapter for some DIY versions.)

KOBE CHEESESTEAK (AKA THE $100 CHEESESTEAK). This marketing gimmick disguised as a food originally featured sautéed foie gras, but when animal rights activists protested, it was replaced by sautéed lobster. The $100 price tag does include a split of Veuve Clicquot champagne that could help you forget what you just paid for a sandwich. Barclay Prime, 237 S. 18th St., 215-732-7560.

VENISON CHEESESTEAK. Venison flank steak covered with truffle cheese, garlic, wild mushrooms, and grilled onions from former Le Bec-Fin chef Daniel Stern's high-end food anchor of Philly's glitzy Cira Centre building. Rae, 2929 Arch St., 215-922-3839.

CHEESESTEAK SPRING ROLL. An upper-end take on a fried cheesesteak treat that first debuted at North Philly Chinese take-outs years ago. Swann Lounge, Four Seasons Hotel, One Logan Square, 215-963-1500; Deuce, 1040 N. Second St., 215-413-3822; Continental, 138 Market St., 215-923-6069.

CHEESESTEAK EMPANADA. Like the above, only *en español*. Bliss, 224 S. Broad St., 215-731-1100; Good Dog, 224 S. 15th St., 215-985-9600.

The Barclay's marketing coup.

CHEESESTEAK BLT. This haute cheesesteak hoagie was named 2007 Best Sandwich in America by NBC's *Today Show*. Vesuvio, 736 S. Eighth St., 215-922-8380.

PHILADELPHIA STYLE STRIP STEAK. The loser in Bobby Flay's Food Network Throwdown with Tony Luke (see page 124). Bobby Flay Steak, 1 Borgata Way, Atlantic City, NJ, 609-317-1000.

George's Sandwich Shop

900 S. NINTH ST., BELLA VISTA, SOUTH PHILADELPHIA, 215-592-8363

There are three calendars inside George's Sandwich Shop: a big girlie one near the cash register, a small religious one by the front window, and a medium-sized one featuring our president near a sink. That might seem excessive in a shop the size of a closet unless you consider that an Onorato family member has been standing at the takeout window of this literal hole-in-the-wall, dishing up almost the exact same hot meat sandwiches, since 1936. Current owner Mark Onorato probably needs reminding that it's the twenty-first century.

If George's menu has stayed largely the same, the pedestrian traffic that prompted Onorato's grandfather, George Vellios, to open this sidewalk equivalent of today's drive-through restaurant lane has diminished greatly since the old days. Before supermarkets and widespread ownership of cars, everyone took the trolley to shop the produce, meat, and fish stands of Ninth Street, and, says Onorato, "a sandwich from here would be a kid's reward for helping their mother or grandmother with their shopping bags."

Now George's is a destination for people who want a literal taste of the past in the form of tripe and barbecue (an Italian kind, made with veal and hot peppers) or George's widely praised roast pork and cheesesteak. Most of

these dishes sit steaming in metal trays below the takeout window, but Onorato makes the cheesesteaks to order with D'Ambrosio rolls that are stacked along the windowsill and Liberty Bell chip steak, a brand owned by one of his cousins. Store founder George's lighthearted grandson, also named George Vellios, owns Lorenzo's Pizza next door and pops in periodically to chat with customers and Onorato. "I like seeing different people, talking to them about different things like we're doing now," says Onorato, forty-nine.

Onorato also clearly likes carrying on a family tradition. Onorato's business card is a replica of his grandfather's, with its 1930s clip art and without a phone number.

ONLY PARTLY ITALIAN, BUT STILL WORTH A STOP

While you're visiting George's, make time to explore its Ninth Street Market home. The so-called Italian Market, on Ninth Street roughly between Christian and Washington, is one of the oldest and largest open-air markets in the country. It originally consisted of Italian immigrants selling Italian produce to other Italian immigrants who missed the fresh fruits and vegetables they enjoyed (and many had actually grown) in the old country.

Almost one hundred years later, most of the Italian vendors are in permanent storefronts that provide some of the street's most interesting culinary browsing: logs of hanging cheese at Di Bruno Brothers and Claudio's, squirming crab at Anastasi Seafood, fresh pasta at Talluto's and Superior, and roast pig that you pick up under the "Roasted Pig Pickup" sign at Cannuli House of Pork. Newer Mexican and Asian immigrants have largely taken over the open-air stands, selling ordinary (and not always local) tomato, lettuce, and eggplant on the street for supercheap (although the real bargains are for large quantities and items that must be eaten immediately). In the fall and winter, these outdoor stand workers still warm up by sidewalk trash can fires. And they don't even occupy the lowest rung in contemporary Italian Market "society." That would be the guys with the hand-lettered signs selling grocery bags or home delivery services via (permanently on loan?) grocery carts and the old Mexican woman who hawks homemade tamales from a chair on the sidewalk. In other words, this is as real a place as it's possible to find in a rapidly gentrifying twenty-first-century Philadelphia.

TO GET THERE: From I-76 E, bear left onto I-676 E/Vine Street Expressway. After about a mile and a half, take the Eighth Street exit and turn right on Eighth. After about a mile and a half, turn right on Montrose Street. Take the first right onto Ninth Street. George's Sandwich Shop is toward the end of the block, to the left. By public transportation, take Bus 47, which stops at Eighth and Christian (walk one block south down Christian).

SEATING: One 8-stool counter. "If there had been 9, we would have had to put in a bathroom," Onorato says.

OFF-STREET PARKING: No

ALCOHOL: No

HOURS: 9 a.m. to 8 p.m. Tuesday through Friday, Saturday until 5 p.m., Sunday until 2 p.m.

ROLL: D'Ambrosio's or unseeded Sarcone's

MEAT: Liberty Bell marinated beef chip steak, cooked to order

ONION: Diced and fresh cooked with the steak

CHEESE: American or provolone

GRILL SEASONING: None

SPECIALTIES: Tripe, barbecued veal, and mild, hot, or Burn My Ass! sausage sandwiches

CELEBRITY STORY: When Sylvester Stallone was on the street filming the first *Rocky*, the then eighteen-year-old Onorato asked for his autograph. Although Stallone was then relatively unknown, according to Onorato, "He said no and jumped in his limo."

Gooey Looie's

PENNSPORT PLAZA, 231 MCCLELLAN ST.,
SOUTH PHILADELPHIA, 215-334-7668

A good many cheesesteaks are dripping, greasy messes. Few steak shops fess up to this quite as forthrightly as Gooey Looie's. Or so it would seem.

When this steak and hoagie shop first opened in 1978, it was an ice cream shop/grocery store/deli. The "gooey" referred to the sauces Looie put on his ice cream sundaes, says current owner Maureen Carbonetta.

When Carbonetta and her then-boyfriend, now-husband Bob bought the business in 1984, they shifted the focus to steaks and hoagies that aren't gooey so much as cheap and so huge that Carbonetta says some people will buy a single steak sandwich and four or five extra rolls and feed the whole family. One single woman told Carbonetta that Gooey Looie hoagie can get her through an entire weekend of meals. That perhaps explains why there are forty-minute waits and lines out the door on Fridays and Saturdays, despite an out-of-the-way courtyard mall location on the site of a former slaughterhouse. (So the Carbonettas' focus on meat is a roots experience of sorts.)

The little shop still has grocery staples along with drinks, chips, and three tiny tables where customers can wait for their made-to-order beefsteaks. Gooey Looie's doesn't sell the chicken kind. Not enough demand. The shop's one bow to healthier eating, a "light" sandwich with half a pound of meat, only seems light compared to its regular steak's 1.35 pounds and is presumably designed for those who want to cap off their cheesesteak with one of the shop's trademark gooey ice cream sundaes.

Maureen Carbonetta

TO GET THERE: From I-76 E, take I-676 E toward Central Philadelphia. Take the Benjamin Franklin Bridge exit, but instead of going on the bridge, stay on Sixth Street. After about two and a quarter miles, turn left at Mifflin. Take the third left onto Moyamensing Avenue, then the second right onto McClellan. Gooey Looie's is located toward the middle of the block, to the right. By public transportation, take Bus 57 to Moyamensing Avenue and Moore Street, then walk one block south on Moyamensing and turn left at McClellan.

SEATING: 3 small tables, barely large enough to hold one of their sandwiches

OFF-STREET PARKING: Yes

ALCOHOL: No

HOURS: 10:30 a.m. to 7 p.m. Monday through Saturday

ROLL: Foot-long D'Ambrosia's

MEAT: Drexel Hill marinated, finely chopped

ONION: Diced, cooked ahead, and then added to the meat as it's cooking on the grill

CHEESE: Six slices of American, provolone, or anything else they have on hand. No Whiz.

GRILL SEASONING: None

SPECIALTIES: Corned beef special (corned beef on rye with Russian dressing and slaw), homemade chicken salad, and unusual ice cream flavors like rum raisin and strawberry cheesecake

CELEBRITY CUSTOMERS: Eagles staff and players, wrestler Blue Meanie, the Fat Boys hip-hop group, and Air Force One (during Bill Clinton's reign)

WEIRDEST ORDERS: A cheesesteak topped with tuna (although grill man Bruce Binck thinks the woman was pregnant) and a steak with onion, mustard, and grape jelly (they had the jelly on hand for breakfast)

Grey Lodge Pub

6235 FRANKFORD AVE., NORTHEAST PHILADELPHIA,
215-825-5357, WWW.GREYLODGE.COM

t's worth going to the Grey Lodge just for the bathrooms. Their broken tile and mirror walls are inspired by local mosaic artist Isaiah Zagar (see page 75), but the Grey Lodge's first-floor men's room walls are also studded with beer caps surrounding snappy beer quotes like "I'd rather have a beer in front of me than a frontal lobotomy."

"Relieving yourself here feels about as right as relieving yourself on the side of the Philadelphia Museum of Art," local writer and Grey Lodge habitué Duane Swierczynski once observed.

However, *Esquire* didn't name Grey Lodge one of the best bars in America for its bathrooms but for its wide and frequently rotating selection of local drafts, mixed-class crowd, offbeat events, and great food, including a cheesesteak that made the top five in WIP radio's 2008 survey (see page 152).

Prior to Mike "Scoats" Scotese's purchase in the mid-1990s, Grey Lodge had been a piano bar with no name and an aging local following. The former computer systems geek dubbed it Grey Lodge for its "manly feel," and because woodsy decorations were easy to come by and cheap, he explains somewhat facetiously. Probe more deeply, though, and he admits the name is partly a comment on *Twin Peaks'* white and black lodges "because life is really grey."

Lodgemaster Scoats

Scoats's interesting mind is also behind offbeat bar events like International Talk Like a Pirate Day (which the bar celebrates with "yo ho ho and a bottle—or two—of Belgian beer, arrr!" and "free, free, free eye patches for any mateys that piratespeak smartly") and the annual Groundhog Day breakfast (in which Wissinoming Winnie—the bar's clay cat answer to Punxsutawney Phil—divines if there will be six more weeks of winter beers or if the spring seasonals will arrive early).

When Scoats added an upstairs kitchen in 2005, he wanted local food to match the local brews. He and food guy Patrick McGinley modeled their cheesesteak on the top-notch slab-style, white-American-sauced products served by the Northeast steakeries surrounding the bar, a few of which Grey Lodge trumped in the WIP contest. Since then, the cheesesteak has become the bar's best-selling food item—and almost as big an attraction as its bathrooms.

TO GET THERE: From I-76 W, take exit 340B/Roosevelt Boulevard and merge onto US-1 N. Bear right and continue for five miles on Roosevelt, then turn right at Devereaux Avenue. After about three-quarters of a mile, turn left at Frankford Avenue. Grey Lodge Pub is located toward the middle of the block, to the right. By public transportation, take the Market-Frankford subway line to Frankford Terminal and take Bus 66 to Harbison and Frankford. Grey Lodge will be about half a block east down Frankford.

SEATING: At 2 bars and some upstairs tables

OFF-STREET PARKING: No

ALCOHOL: Definitely—especially strong in draft beers and whiskeys

HOURS: 11 a.m. to midnight Monday through Thursday, until 1 a.m. Friday and Saturday, until 11 p.m. Sunday

ROLL: DePalma's

MEAT: Rib-eye, thin-sliced, slab-style

ONION: Spanish, chopped into inch-sized squares and sautéed until brown and sweet

CHEESE: White American mixed with whole milk to make a sauce, or provolone

GRILL SEASONING: None

SPECIALTIES: Twice-cooked fries named Best of Philly in *Philadelphia* magazine in 2007

Grilladelphia

EXXON TIGER MART, 2330 ARAMINGO AVE., KENSINGTON, PHILADELPHIA, 215-739-3807, WWW.GRILLADELPHIA.COM

Atmosphere-wise, cheesesteak shops are generally pretty humble. But few are as unpretentious as Grilladelphia's location inside a gas station. Let's just say you might not want to suggest it for your first Match.com meeting.

Grilladelphia/Exxon Tiger Mart owner Barry Appelbaum has fond memories of eating at the long-defunct Mike and Carol's stand at Ninth and Wharton as a kid and speaks of Steve of Steve's Prince of Steak in reverential tones. But the origins of his unusual idea had more to do with money than love. All those $100 tank-fills mostly go into the pockets of Big Oil, Applebaum says. A small-time gas station owner like him has to do food service in order to survive. But McDonald's and Subway do miserably inside gas stations in Philly, mainly because, as Applebaum says, "every corner pizza shop here also makes steaks, subs, and hoagies—and they deliver."

So Applebaum decided to create his own quick-service restaurant with a product so unique and good that people would come even when they had enough gas to get home. Hence the Exxon Tiger Mart's Grilladelphia, a cheesesteakery serving made-to-order steaks in distinctive Italian pouch rolls. Not only are these hollowed-out rolls unique, but they make a dripping cheesesteak neater and easier to eat in a car or truck, the preferred eating venue for most of Grilladelphia's customers. Those who do elect to eat at the six-stool counter will find an atmosphere reminiscent of a diner. There are permanently piped-in doo-wop tunes but none of the usual steak shop celebrity pictures. No matter. Probably the most important local celebrity for a food business did visit, and *Philadelphia Inquirer* restaurant critic Craig LaBan called Grilladelphia "a serious steakery" shortly afterward.

So quality isn't the problem. But profitability has been challenged by the rising costs of flour and beef—money Applebaum is trying to get back by training all staff members to make the sandwiches, meaning you can get one even in the wee hours when there are only a few people working.

The thirty-year gas station vet also curses the day the gas pumps were designed to accept credit cards—thus eliminating the need for people to walk into his store. But his biggest problem remains his location. "People find it hard to believe that good food could come out of a gas station," he says with a sigh.

> ## "a serious steakery"
> —Craig LaBan

Barry Applebaum showing off his buns

TO GET THERE: From I-95 N, take the Girard Avenue/Lehigh Avenue exit onto Delaware Avenue, bear left onto Aramingo. take the first left onto York and then an immediate left into the Tiger Mart driveway. By public transportation, take the Market-Frankford subway line to the Girard stop and take Bus 15 to Girard and Susquehanna, then walk a quarter of a mile northeast up Aramingo. Or take the Market-Frankford subway line to the Spring Garden stop and take Bus 43 to York and Aramingo, then walk southwest down Aramingo.

SEATING: For 6

OFF-STREET PARKING: Yes

ALCOHOL: No

HOURS: 24/7

ROLL: Unique Italian pouch first used by the now defunct Piccolo's Bar in the Northeast and now handmade for Applebaum by Dan Vilotti of D'Ambrosio's

MEAT: Beef loin from Liberty Bell Steak, chopped-style

ONION: Sliced thin and cooked with the meat

CHEESE: American, provolone, or Whiz, all melted on the meat on the grill

GRILL SEASONING: Water only

Ishkabibble's

337 SOUTH ST., CENTER CITY,
PHILADELPHIA, 215-923-4337

With its hand-painted pink and black storefront, signature Gremlin drink, and wacky name, Ishkabibble's is about as funky as South Street gets these days.

Old-timers will tell you that it's not half as funky as it used to be. One week in the mid-1970s, the Ishkabibble's building was the site of Ed Beckerman and Joel Spivak's "breakfast club," morning get-togethers for friends and neighbors that rewarded anyone who slept overnight in the storefront window with breakfast in bed—or at least, most people slept. The buddies were also known for their semiregular National Hash Day celebrations (with hashish cake, naturally) and Miss Slum Goddess contest (once won by a transsexual bartender from the nearby Lickety Split who declared herself "the embodiment of the Renaissance").

Beckerman also ran a sort of regular restaurant there in 1976 called E. S. Eddie's, which stood for Eat S--- Eddie's; the offensive name was derived from one disappointed patron's description of Eddie's fare. The name restaurateur Bart Brown gave the place when he took over in 1979 was similarly whimsical and so mysterious that current owner Young Ahn has created a laminated FAQ sheet to answer all the questions. Ask for it and you'll find out that Ishkabbible (pronounced *ish* as in *wish* and *bib* as in something you might wish to wear while eating a messy cheesesteak) has several meanings. It is a Yiddish expression meaning something like "Do I look like I care?" It is also the title of a 1913 song and the nickname of big band trumpeter Merwyn Bogue, who sang that song and other novelty tunes in the Kay Kayser big band of the 1930s and 1940s. Bogue had a bowl haircut and wore silly hats—hence the propellered beanie on the Philadelphia Ishkabibble's logo.

Ishkabibble's was among the first places in the city to serve chicken cheesesteaks (if not *the* first as they claim—see next page for more) and it still sells as many of them as beef (and many more than most steak stands). Ishkabbible's is also famous for their half-lemonade, half-grape-juice Gremlin drink and freshly made Spanish fries (which are french fries topped with hot peppers and onions).

Ishkabbible's is located right across the street from the Theater of the Living Arts rock club, and the left wall of the tiny stand is covered with signed framed photos of musicians, including one of the trumpeter Ish Kabibble, inscribed with thanks to Brown for "keeping my name alive."

Ahn is doing his best to keep Ishkabibble's traditions alive, although he was powerless to stop 2008 sidewalk work from felling the storefront tree that generations of South Street teens had decorated with their used chewing gum.

Ishkabibble's owner Young Ahn

TO GET THERE: Take the South Street exit off I-76 E. Turn left at South Street and go about two miles. Ishkabibble's is located on the left between Fourth and Orianna. By public transportation from Center City, take Bus 32 and get off at Lombard and South or take Bus 33 to Market and Fourth and walk about three-quarters of a mile south down Fourth.

OTHER LOCATIONS: A Ninth and Federal branch that was near Geno's and Pat's closed in 2002 and is now Mexican eatery La Lupe.

SEATING: For 9 between two small counters. Most of the business is from the takeout window.

OFF-STREET PARKING: No

ALCOHOL: No

HOURS: 9 a.m. to 11 p.m. Sunday through Thursday, until 2 a.m. Friday and Saturday

ROLL: Won't disclose (although there are Liscio's boxes in the shop)

MEAT: Extra lean loin tail, chopped

ONION: Chopped and cooked with the meat

CHEESE: American, Whiz, or provolone

GRILL SEASONING: A little vegetable oil

SPECIALTIES: Gremlin drink, Spanish and sweet potato fries, and chicken cheesesteak made with chunks of chicken tenders

THE CHICKEN CHEESESTEAK'S REAL FATHER (I THINK)

Ishkabibble's is only one of several steak shops that claim to have invented the chicken cheesesteak. But Ed Cohen says it was really "Schultzy" of West Philly sandwich shop Billy Bob's in the early 1980s, and he should know: Bill Schultz's invention was the inspiration for the pioneering chicken cheesesteak wholesale business Cohen started with Alvin Shipon.

Prior to that, Cohen had been a wholesale food supplier and Billy Bob's manager Bill Schultz was one of his customers. One day Cohen noticed that Schultz had frozen some chicken breast in metal pans.

Schultz takes up the story from there: "We were right on the Penn campus, so our customers were a little more educated and interested in eating a little healthier. I started playing around with chicken, freezing it, pulling it out to temper it, and then slicing it the same way I did

Bill Schultz with his invention

with beef for regular cheesesteaks."

Schultz put up a sign, "New Chicken Steaks," and sold twenty to thirty the first day. Within a week or two, he was selling two hundred a day. "It was a monster," Schultz recalls.

Initially the chicken sandwich was not very popular. Shultz says, "I can't tell you how many people threw me out. It didn't fit the Philly macho image. A lot of them didn't care that it might be healthier."

Cohen's initial attempts to sell a copycat chicken steak to other restaurants were much less successful. Cohen says, "I can't tell you how many people threw me out. It didn't fit the Philly macho image." Now, of course, all but the oldest and most traditional steak shops offer a chicken option. And you can still try the original at Schultz's Victoria's Pizza parlor in Northeast Philly.

Jim's Steaks

400 SOUTH ST., CENTER CITY, PHILADELPHIA, 215-928-1911, WWW.JIMSTEAKS.COM

The grimier, the more uncomfortable the surroundings, the better the steaks, is the general unwritten rule of cheesesteakdom.

If so, Jim's Steaks breaks it. Jim's is clean, has seating, and even has some architectural style. No wonder the tourists go there in rolling rivers of Cheez Whiz. The other reason is Jim's location on South Street, the Fisherman's Wharf or Vegas Strip of Philly (that is, a place with pedestrian traffic at all hours of the day and night).

Guides on the tourist duck boats that cruise down South Street say Jim's dates back to 1939—the liars. This Jim's is actually a safer, mid-1970s spin-off of the original Jim's on North Sixty-second Street, a place where out-of-towners now rightly fear to tread. Back in 1939, that part of West Philadelphia was a mixed neighborhood of Italians, Irish, and blacks with a Catholic school whose students would snack on the candy and soda Millie Pearlingi began selling from the front window of her row house to supplement the roofer income of her husband, Jim.

Jim's owner Abner Silver (left) with employee Tony Ryder

Before long, Jim and Millie's menu expanded to takeout lunch items, including steak sandwiches made with top and bottom round that became so popular that Jim was able to quit his roofing job and the family had to find some other place to live.

The spiffy black, white, and chrome art deco architecture of all four Jim's Steaks restaurants is not original to the first Jim's, as many people assume. Art deco had all but died out by the late 1930s and in any case was much too fancy and expensive for Depression-era blue-collar Philadelphia. Current Jim's owner Bill Proetto ordered the chainwide redesign when he opened the South Street shop in the mid-1970s to give his cheesesteak patrons the same "zippy" feeling he gets from his personal deco collection, including fifty Louis Icarts and twenty Maxfield Parrishes. Many people associate the look with diners: Jim's is just cleaner and nicer to its patrons than most diners (or cheesesteak places). During peak dining hours

Founders Millie and Jim (upper right) and family

JIM'S STEAKS HOAGIES

The original Sixty-second Street Jim's

one employee does nothing but tidy up the tiny upstairs dining room. A sign up there thanks people for "not saving seats while others are waiting for their food." (Compare that to the one at Pat's banishing ordering miscreants to the back of the line.)

To get to the upstairs seating area, diners have to pass through a hallway containing boxes of Amoroso's rolls, industrial-size Cheez Whiz cans, and a machine where an employee slices top round steak to paper-thinness. In other words, everything's out in the open, including the lard and oil blend Jim's uses in cooking the meat. "It gives a wonderful flavor. I'll bet Le Bec-Fin uses it too," says co-owner Abner Silver, referring to Philly's most haute French restaurant.

The silver-haired Silver, a jazz buff, is responsible for the unusually large number of local and national jazz figures among the signed celebrity pictures that decorate the walls along with tributes to cheesesteak-eating champs. The current record—thirteen in fifty-seven minutes set in 2007 by a Royersford, Pennsylvania, IT manager—makes the hefty eleven-incher most people eat seem like a little snack.

TO GET THERE: From I-76 E, take the South Street exit. Turn left at South Street and go about two miles. Jim's is located at the intersection of Fourth and South, to the right. By public transportation, take any Regional Rail to the Market East Station; walk seven blocks east to Fourth Street and then seven blocks south on Fourth to South Street. By public transportation from Center City, take Bus 32 and get off at Lombard and South, or take Bus 33 to Market and Fourth and walk about three-quarters of a mile south down Fourth.

OTHER LOCATIONS: 431 N. 62nd St., West Philadelphia, 215-747-6617 (original shop); 2311 Cottman Ave., Northeast Philadelphia, 215-333-5467; 469 Baltimore Pike, Springfield, 610-544-8400

SEATING: At a counter downstairs and tables upstairs

OFF-STREET PARKING: No

ALCOHOL: Yes, decent bottled beer selection

HOURS: 10 a.m. to 1 or 2 a.m. Monday through Saturday, noon to 10 p.m. Sunday

ROLL: 11-inch Amoroso's

MEAT: Prime or choice U.S. steer top round, sliced in-house and chopped on the grill (Jim's being the only representative of the chopped-style steak among the city's highest-volume shops)

ONION: Chopped and precooked

CHEESE: Whiz, provolone, or American

GRILL SEASONING: Lard-containing Divo brand oil blend and a secret spice Abner Silver won't reveal. (Could it be the same one used at his old Abner's? See page 35.)

CELEBRITY STORIES: Singer Lou Rawls showed up at South Street one evening and told staff that he had been "driving around for hours trying to find the place." "Get to the back of the line," ordered the unimpressed manager.

After downing a sandwich in the celebrity-photo-adorned upstairs dining room, a scruffy-looking man asked the meat cutter if the shop would like an autograph. "Who are you?" the cutter asked. Not being a folk music fan, the cutter didn't recognize the name Dylan. "Have you ever been on [Johnny] Carson?" he asked. When Dylan said no, the cutter said he would take him up on his offer if he ever was.

PHILLY TACO
(THE JIM'S/LORENZO CHALLENGE)

Not up to breaking the current Jim's eating record of thirteen sandwiches an hour? You might want to instead opt for the fun run of South Street competitive cheesesteak eating, the so-called Philly taco. This is a Jim's cheesesteak rolled up in a slice from Lorenzo and Sons pizza just up the street. Yes, I know this sounds more like a burrito. But don't try logic on the inebriated types who usually take up this challenge. (Note: An Ishkabibble's or Steaks on South cheesesteak is an acceptable substitute if the lines at Jim's are too long.)

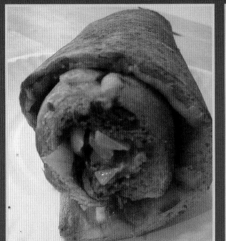

The Philly Taco: two junk food treats in one

WOULD YOU LIKE ART WITH THAT?

Once finished enjoying the culinary and deco arts at Jim's, art buffs will want to check out the tile-and-mirror mosaics decorating the Eyes Gallery building next door. They're the work of Isaiah Zagar, a local folk artist whose signature blend of colored cement, cut mirror, ceramic, and tile adorn so many public buildings and private homes around town that Zagar mosaics have become the Philly equivalent of San Francisco's painted ladies. Want to see more? Walk six blocks west to 1024 South Street and visit Zagar's Magic Gardens, a labyrinthine collection of decorated surfaces and sculpture and just plain junk showcased (fans say transformed) by the artist's vision.

Johnny's Hots

1234 N. DELAWARE AVE., FISHTOWN,
PHILADELPHIA, 215-423-2280
(ALTHOUGH THEY RARELY ANSWER),
WWW.JOHNNYSHOTS.COM

Being the best sausage sandwich guy in Philadelphia is sort of like making the best crab cake in Houston: it's good but a little irrelevant. If you want big business and widespread acclaim in Philly, you have to make a great cheesesteak.

Johnny's Hots' stand was selling sausages for fifty years before they added cheesesteaks to the menu. Within a year of their 2005 introduction, Johnny's Hots' cheesesteaks beat Pat's, Geno's, Tony Luke's, and all the rest to win *Philadelphia* magazine's coveted best cheesesteak prize.

Johnny's Hots debuted as a humble hot dog and sausage truck at the corner of Delaware Avenue and Poplar Street in 1955. But after being hassled by a neighboring dinner theater that saw him as competition, Nunzio "Johnny" Danze moved his business to an even more modest Pier 35½ scrap metal yard shack. How modest was it? In the winter they had to keep a portable heater running all night to keep the water pipes and propane flowing. But the scrap metal dealer said a sale was imminent, so he wouldn't let Danze fix the place up.

Forty years later, with that sale finally seeming likely, Johnny's son, current owner John Danze, bought the old Peg's diner right up the street and began renovations. Although the new Johnny's is still a takeout stand, it's much bigger and spiffier—especially inside, where Danze splurged on a fifteen-foot chrome-plated grill.

Danze started thinking about adding steaks to the menu partly as a way to pay for the new place. He spent six months trying out different steak meats. As "the new guy, I had to be better," Danze reasoned. That ruled out the rib-eye most shops use. He personally thought chuck had the best flavor, but he said that the visible fat made some of his customers "think it was cheap." Prime top round from the nearby Kissin Fresh Meats was the compromise. It's hanging beef ("the kind Rocky boxed," Danze notes) that Kissin cuts up and Danze slices. Cooked to order with onions, then placed in a Liscio's hoagie roll, this steak has proven so popular that it has knocked Johnny's Hots' pork sandwich out of its longtime spot as second-best seller. (The hot sausages remain number one.) Danze says that since adding the cheesesteaks and Saturday hours, business has doubled.

And if current plans to build the SugarHouse Casino just around the bend go through as planned, Johnny's Hots' already hot business should get even hotter.

John Danze at his Cadillac of a grill

STORY: One day in 1999, a car careened off Delaware Avenue toward the old Johnny's Hots shack. The lunchtime line scattered and John Danze and his sister crouched behind the refrigerator. But when the car hit the building next door, everyone quickly got back in line. And after the driver was taken to the hospital, Danze says he got "quite a bit of business from the fire department crew."

TO GET THERE: From I-95 N, take the Girard Avenue/Lehigh Avenue exit onto Delaware. Bear left to stay on Delaware (following the signs for Aramingo). After half a mile, take a sharp left and go under the overpass. Johnny Hots is located toward the middle of the block, to the right. By public transportation, take the Market-Frankford subway line to the Girard stop and take Bus 15 to Girard and Marlborough. From there, walk a quarter of a mile southeast down Marlborough, then turn left on Delaware.

SEATING: One park bench, along with some stand-up metal counters surrounding the building's support poles

OFF-STREET PARKING: A small lot

ALCOHOL: No

HOURS: 5 a.m. to 3 p.m. Monday through Friday, 7 a.m. to 2 p.m. Saturday

ROLL: Liscio's 12-inch hoagie

MEAT: Top round, sliced thin on-site and cooked to order

ONION: Hand-diced (machines make them gloppy, Danze says) and cooked with the steaks

CHEESE: Whiz, white American, or provolone

GRILL SEASONING: Olive oil

SPECIALTIES: The shop's namesake hot Polish beef sausage sandwich, old-fashioned Philadelphia "surf and turf" combo consisting of a mashed fish cake served atop a split grilled hot dog, and pork sandwich with greens and provolone cheese

STORY: In March 2008 a Johnny's Hots hot sausage sandwich was credited with helping Philadelphia avert a potentially catastrophic bridge collapse on I-95. Structural engineer Peter Kim and partner Tony Jen stopped at Johnny's Hots for a late lunch. After eating the sandwiches in the car, they drove north on Richmond Street below I-95, where Kim spotted a huge crack in a six-lane bridge column. He called Pennsylvania Department of Transportation officials and the bridge was ordered closed immediately. Despite traffic jams that clogged Delaware Avenue in front of Johnny's Hots, the stand did not end up financially benefiting from its savior role. "People don't stop in a traffic jam; all they want to do is get home," says Danze.

John's Roast Pork

14 E. SNYDER AVE., SOUTH PHILADELPHIA
215-463-1951, WWW.JOHNSROASTPORK.COM

"My in-laws started in a little wooden shack, and now we have a cinder block shack."

What's the best cheesesteak place? Philadelphians discuss this question with as much passion and frequency as people elsewhere talk about their favorite sports team, music group, or TV show. And nowadays the most impartial answer to that question would be John's Roast Pork. John's cheesesteak came in first in multiple-stand surveys by WIP sports radio host Glen Macnow and *Philadelphia Inquirer* restaurant critic Craig LaBan (who also once said he'd go to John's for his last meal). It even got a citation from the la-di-da James Beard Foundation. This, for what most people don't even believe is John's best sandwich. (That would be the namesake roast pork—see page 81.)

Vonda Bucci sums up John's Roast Pork's history thusly: "My in-laws started in a little wooden shack, and now we have a cinder block shack." To be a bit more specific, Vonda's father-in-law, Domenico Bucci, began selling roast pork sandwiches from his secret two-day recipe out of a walk-up wooden stand by the railroad tracks in 1930. Blue-collar workers from the nearby alcohol distillery and shipyard were his main customers until those places closed, ushering in a long fallow 1980s for Bucci's son, stand namesake

John, before the big box stores moved in with their new local customers. Certainly no tourists ever got this deep into South Philly.

At least, that was the case until the early 2000s, when critic LaBan's praise—first for John's pork sandwich, then for the cheesesteaks John's son added in 1978—set off a chain reaction of media mentions and increased business, culminating in John's triple-crown win during radio man Macnow's 2008 cheesesteak survey. Not only was John's cheesesteak Macnow's favorite, but it also placed first with the celebrity judges and the public at Macnow's culminating May 2008 taste-off (see page 152.)

Why does John's cheesesteak win everything? "Because we make the sandwiches like we would if we were going to eat them," says Vonda Bucci, seventy-five. That means serving up a generous twelve ounces of shop-cut rib-eye and five slices of American cheese on a brawny roll from the nearby Carangi Bakery that can be ordered with or with-out sesame seeds—thereby adding a whole new flavor dimension, not to mention a new meaning to the phrase "cheesesteak wit." Whiz is not an option at John's, by the way. "We don't like it, so we don't serve it," states the characteristically blunt Vonda.

Folks obviously must like having cheesesteaks Vonda's way; as late as 2 p.m. one recent weekday, a long of line of hungry people snaked through the tiny space with the help of a movie-theater-style crowd control rope and "guidance" from Vonda. "Keep moving! Order your sandwiches! Step down!" she regularly bellows from her perch at the cash register.

Following the financial reckoning, the sandwich-laden diners are spewed out onto a patio with half a dozen cement-bolted picnic tables and a view of the worst of Philly landscapes old and new. To the south are railroad tracks and a smoke-belching chemical plant; to the north are a ShopRite, IHOP, and Target. And yet the place is so popular that strangers regularly must share tables.

TO GET THERE: From I-95 S, take the Walt Whitman Bridge/Packer Avenue exit toward Oregon Avenue. Turn left onto Front Street, then right onto Oregon, the first major intersection. Immediately after the overpass, turn left on Swanson and go down half a mile. Turn right at Snyder, where John's Roast Pork is located to the right. By public transportation, take Bus 57 to Fourth and Snyder and walk half a mile east on Snyder. Or take Bus 25 to Pier 70 (Moore and Swanson), walk about a quarter of a mile south down Swanson, then turn left onto Snyder.

SEATING: 9 outdoor tables

OFF-STREET PARKING: No

ALCOHOL: No

HOURS: 6:45 a.m. to 3 p.m. Monday through Friday (grill closes at 2:30 p.m.)

ROLL: 24-inch Carangi loaf cut in half

MEAT: Steer rib-eye, sliced paper-thin on the premises, cooked to order, and lightly chopped

ONION: Chopped and precooked

CHEESE: American or provolone (mild or sharp), melted on the meat on the grill

GRILL SEASONING: Oil, salt, and pepper

SPECIALTIES: Roast pork sandwich with provolone and spinach, and bruschetta cheesesteak (garlic, basil, tomato, and olive oil with the steak and onion)

Sadly, in summer 2008, third-generation owner John Bucci Jr. was not at the shop to enjoy its hard-won success. John, who took over the cooking chores when his father died of cancer in 1991, was instead recovering from a bone marrow transplant performed to ward off leukemia. If all goes well, he might be able to return to work in a year. In the meantime, other Buccis are filling in.

"We are not a franchise. We're run by family," Vonda says in answer to a question about the place's popularity. When asked if people like to support family businesses, Vonda replies, "They could care. They just like a good sandwich."

CONSIDERING THE ALTERNATIVE (THE GREAT PHILLY ROAST PORK)

Visitors come to Philadelphia looking for the best cheesesteak. But those who want Philadelphia's best hot sandwich might actually want to order the roast pork. At the very least, they should consider ordering a roast pork sandwich alongside a cheesesteak.

Fortunately, the sandwiches' common Italian immigrant roots mean some of the best places to get the former are also among the best places to get the latter, including John's Roast Pork, Tony Luke's (see page 122), and DiNic's (which doesn't sell cheesesteaks but is located right across the aisle in the Reading Terminal Market from a place that does—Spataro's, see page 111). If you're like most people, you'll enjoy the cheesesteak and fall in love with the roast pork.

That could be because this combination of seasoned, slow-roasted pork, provolone cheese, and garlicky sautéed greens placed in a hearty Italian roll with some of its roasting juices is a lot more complex in taste and texture. It also takes a lot more time and trouble to make: the premier roast pork makers slow-roast their hams for one to two days. Choose the broccoli rabe instead of the milder spinach and you will even taste some bitterness. Kids will hate it and so will many others: the blander, more straightforward cheesesteak is universally pleasing. But if you've moved from Britney to Miles in music, and from Grisham to Joyce in your reading, you just might be ready to try the roast pork.

STAKING OUT THE STEAK

Pat Olivieri made the world's first steak sandwich with a piece of hand-sliced rib-eye beef. Today Pat's is one of a handful of Philly area shops—Steve's Prince of Steaks, Geno's, Philip's, John's House of Pork, and Claymont Steak Shop are some others—that slices their own rib-eye on-premises. (Jim's cuts its own top round, which is a little leaner cut of meat with a different flavor.)

But the time, expense, and safety issues involved with thin-slicing steaks means that the majority of steak shops let butchers or meat processors slice their meat for them and sometimes re-form, marinate, and flavor it too. After 1950 dozens of meat companies sprang up or opened new divisions to serve the Philly steak market, including current major players the Original Philadelphia Cheesesteak Company, Liberty Bell Steak Company, Drexel Foods, and Astra Foods, all located in Greater Philly, and Advance Food Company of Oklahoma.

As with any "natural" food, the quality of unadulterated rib-eye can vary depending on the breed of animal it comes from and what the animal ate. It ranges from the cheap, tough milk cow beef Pat Olivieri probably first used during the Depression to the prime aged steer rib-eye served at the high-end Palm Restaurant chain.

Almost all grades of rib-eye contain a fair amount of fat. Fat gives meat a lot of flavor, but those white streaks can be off-putting when customers are watching the meat cook, as is the custom in steak shops. Even worse is when the fat manifests itself as strings of gristle or "rubber bands," as they're known in the business. By most accounts, the chopped-style of cheesesteak meat had its origins in grill chefs trying to eliminate or disguise tough pieces like these (although over time it has evolved into a serving preference).

Tommy on meat-cutting duty at Philip's

Rib-eye is still more expensive than comparable top round or sirloin, and all these large "whole muscle" steaks are more expensive than smaller chunks and trimmings. Hence the birth of the "chopped and formed" steak: smaller or otherwise more problematic pieces of rib, loin, round and/or brisket are chopped into Ping-Pong- to tennis-ball-sized chunks, mixed in big defect-distributing batches, and then molded into thin steak slices.

Sound delicious? It depends on the meat. The sirloin tip, loin tails, and rib lifter meat now commonly used in chopped and formed products can be up to 94 percent lean and are therefore less flavorful than the fattier rib-eye. Marinades can help correct that and also prevent the meat from drying out in restaurants where it's cooked in batches and kept sitting on the grill. Marinades also act as a meat extender, further lowering the price. No wonder these products are popular. Although the Original Philadelphia Cheesesteak Company sells dozens of Philly steak products, including an unadulterated sliced rib-eye, 40 to 50 percent of all that company's business now comes from a chopped and formed, marinated and seasoned loin tail/rib lifter product called WOW (which was a customer's reaction on first trying it). In a bow to tradition, the company even makes a four-ounce rib-eye-shaped version.

Pizza shop owners and lunch truck operators who want to save even more money serve emulsified steak products, which are even more processed. These can legally be made from virtually any piece of the cow, which is chopped and then finely ground into pastelike hamburger—except that in this case the paste is molded and sliced. Like hamburger, these steaks can contain up to 30 percent fat. Emulsified products make up the majority of the frozen minute (a.k.a. sandwich steaks) sold in the supermarket freezer case.

But how do you know what meat you're getting when you order a cheesesteak from a restaurant or stand? You can't unless it's a place profiled in this book or you see slicing machines or a box with an identifying label. But the price and the cooking presentation can offer clues. If the cook is chopping the meat like crazy and the shop is charging $4.50 a sandwich, it's a safe bet the place is *not* using The Palm's meat purveyor.

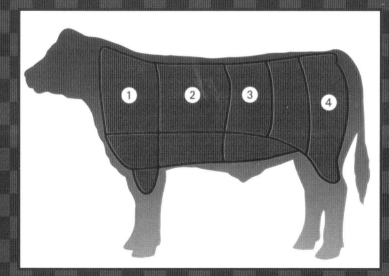

Pinning your Steak Sandwich on the Steer Body Part: 1. chuck eye roast; 2. rib-eye steak, rib lifter; 3. loin tail; and 4. top and bottom round and sirloin tip

Larry's Steaks

2459 N. 54TH ST., BALA CYNWYD, PHILADELPHIA, 215-879-1776, WWW.LARRYSSTEAKS.COM

Larry's is to St. Joseph's University what Abner's is to the University of Pennsylvania and Drexel: the unofficial college cheesesteak stand and, for these students, the measure of what a cheesesteak should be forever after. And mainly what St. Joe's students and alums think cheesesteaks should be is big.

"Betcha can't eat one"

Larry's also shares Abner's association with local sports teams (in Larry's case, St. Joe's and the 76ers, who used to practice in a field house across the street). The two shops are even laid out alike, with a grill in the left front, lots of seating, and permanently-set-to-sports big-screen TVs.

Larry Morroney actually started his namesake steak business at Sixtieth Street and Lancaster Avenue in 1955. Four years later, he launched his signature Belly Filler—one and a quarter pounds of rib-eye beef on a three-foot-long roll. "Betcha can't eat one," Larry's menu has taunted ever since, although the winner of a mid-1990s Belly Filler–eating contest between St. Joe's and Villanova colleges stuffed down four and a half.

The sandwiches are filled from the enormous pile of meat that sits on the right side of Larry's front-window grill, awaiting the hordes that rush in after afternoon classes. For years, Larry's was also known for sturdy paper cups covered with Larry aphorisms like "Everybody has something to offer." And Larry's son, Michael Morroney, says his dad lived up to them. "He liked everybody and could talk to anybody, from a college president to a mechanic."

Larry opened the Fifty-fourth Street shop in 1972 and ran it until his death in 1985. In 1990 the business was purchased by Egyptian Tony Elebah, who also owns Broad Street's Oak Lane Diner. Elebah was behind the 2000 pastel-color renovation, which gives Larry's its current casual dining, chain-restaurant feel, and the new logo featuring a sliced globe serving as a roll for hoagie meats and cheeses—reflecting Elebah's international perspective or suggesting that Larry's food is world renowned or maybe both.

What remains from Morroney days are the Belly Buster and the "QQQ??? Always Ask" menu note. But don't ask what it means: neither Elebah nor Michael Morroney remember.

TO GET THERE: From I-76 W, take exit 339/City Avenue, bear right, and merge onto City Avenue/US-1 S. After a mile and a half, turn left at 54th Street. Larry's Steaks is located toward the middle of the block, to the left. By public transportation, take Bus 44 to Overbrook and 54th. Or take Bus 124 or Bus 125 to the Wissahickon Transfer Station and transfer to Bus 1, which also stops at Overbrook and 54th. From there, stay on the right side of the street and walk north up 54th.

SEATING: Seating for 75 at tables and booths

OFF-STREET PARKING: No

ALCOHOL: No

HOURS: 10 a.m. to 2 or 3 a.m. Monday through Saturday, 11 a.m. to 11 p.m. Sunday

ROLL: Amoroso's, specially made for Larry's

MEAT: Steer rib-eye, chopped, cooked in batches, and piled up in a mountain

ONION: Diced and cooked in batches

CHEESE: Provolone, thick-cut white American, or Cheez Whiz placed on the bread

GRILL SEASONING: Water only

CELEBRITY STORY: Larry Morroney's son, Michael, remembers the day Muhammad Ali visited his father's steak shop. Michael says, "He had just bought a mansion near Haverford and he walked in with his whole entourage. He was six foot five and absolutely handsome."

It was in the mid-1960s, shortly after Ali had become a Muslim and changed his name. Michael recalls, "I didn't know what to call him so I just said, 'Champ, I will make you a feast for your mouth.' He said, 'I can't eat no pork.' I said, 'Don't you worry.' I made him a mushroom cheesesteak and he almost ate the paper plate."

CHEESESTEAK INVENTOR CLAIM: Larry Morroney's son, Michael, is one of several people who claim to have invented the cheesesteak. Morroney says that when his dad opened Larry's Steaks in 1955, "There was no such thing as a cheesesteak." But Larry's did sell cheeseburgers. One day in 1957 while working there, he tried the same cheese on a steak sandwich, and before long, more and more customers were asking for it that way. "To my knowledge, I was the first," he says.

Leo's Steaks

1403 CHESTER PIKE, FOLCROFT, 215-586-1199

People are always saying "you can't miss it" about places that are impossible to find. But that statement is no lie about Leo's, a huge pink elephant of a stucco building serving up almost-as-big steaks.

At least it's big outside. Inside customers wait for their orders in the same tiny potato-chip-rack-and-soda-case-stuffed space as every other steak shop. (It's as if there were some kind of rule that no authentic Philly area cheesesteak shop's interior can be larger than 12 x 12 feet.) But Leo's co-owner Jack Mullan says in this case it's because most of Leo's building is taken up by apartments (for the deaf, I assume, since the clanging from the chopping of the steak meat at Leo's is so loud you can hear it from the street).

The small waiting space might also be Jack and his partner-brothers' way of recreating the cozy feeling they had when the shop first opened in a 10 x 10-foot former trolley shack next to the trolley tracks across the street. Jack's brother Leo opened the place as a produce stand in 1972; steaks were added two years later to bolster winter business. That space was so small, Jack recalls, employees who went up to the

Leo's brother Jack

second floor to do prep work had to shout down for permission to come back down. "If there were more than a few customers, there literally wouldn't be room," he says.

The business moved to its current location in 1987 when the local public transportation agency decided to turn the little building back into a trolley stop. By then, Leo was long gone, having been replaced in the business by brother Stephen. (Jack will not elucidate the reason.) The Mullans' father, also named Leo, actually opened a competing Leo's steak shop just down the street from his son's place in the late 1990s, but when you suggest this might have been a source of family discord, Jack counters, "Actually, we used to help him out, and we shared our help back and forth when someone didn't come in."

"Both Leos are dead now," Jack continues, in a way that doesn't invite further questions. The three remaining brothers—Jack, Stephen, and Bill—now take turns running the business.

Jack recently got a call from a guy seeking advice on starting a cheesesteak place in Texas. Jack says, "I told him, 'It's great if you want to work twenty-four hours a day, seven days a week.' People think it's like Puff the Magic Dragon—the tomatoes, the rolls—that they just magically appear. But it's all work—from every little detail to every big decision."

Fortunately for Leo's Steaks, the family's hard work has been recognized with dozens of best cheesesteak awards, including two from *Philadelphia* magazine. Jack says they're partly a result of how "we never weigh up a sandwich—we just make sure they're packed." Guys boast of having eaten two of Leo's eighteen-inchers, but Jack says, "I've never seen it." Even one is enough to put people away for the day. He adds, "They think they're going back to work, but then I'll see them out there in their cars asleep."

Leo (center) at the 1979 Chicago travel fair

TO GET THERE: From I-95 N, take the Ridley Park exit. Turn left at Stewart Avenue, then right on US-13/Chester Pike. Go about three and a half miles. Leo's Steaks is located at the corner of Burton Lane and Chester Pike, to the right. By public transportation, take Regional Rail R2 to Folcroft/Sharon Hill stop, walk northwest down Primos Avenue for about a quarter of a mile, then turn right on Chester and walk about a quarter of a mile. Or take the Market-Frankford subway line to the 69th Street terminal and take Trolley 102 to Sharon Hill. From there, walk one block southwest down Chester.

SEATING: 2 picnic tables outside

OFF-STREET PARKING: No

ALCOHOL: No

HOURS: 10 a.m. to 11 p.m. or midnight Monday through Saturday, until 9 p.m. Sunday

ROLL: Amoroso's

MEAT: Rib-eye, vigorously chopped

ONION: Chopped and cooked with the meat

CHEESE: American, provolone, or Swiss. Says Jack Mullan, "We do not allow Cheez Whiz in the store. It's too far down on the scale of foods in our opinion."

GRILL SEASONING: None

STORY: In 1979 United Airlines flew the Mullan brothers to Chicago to serve Philly's most famous sandwich at a travel fair. Jack Mullan says no one had any idea what a cheesesteak was. "It was like we were coming from outer space. Steak shops weren't that big then. It's different now."

LOU'S

414 E. MAIN ST., NORRISTOWN, 610-279-5415

Philadelphians have almost as many rules for sub sandwiches as they do for cheesesteaks. For one thing, they're not called subs: They're hoagies. For another, they never have mustard and they're never served warm.

Got that? Now forget it. Because the industrial Philly ring city of Norristown, the home of Lou's, is the one place in the world where cold sandwiches are called zeps (for their airship-like shape) and feature a single set of ingredients: cooked salami, tomato, provolone cheese, onions, tomato, oil, and oregano (but never lettuce).

Lou's is best-known for its zeps. But steaks come next. Co-owner Charles Alba says it's because they're made to order on fresh rolls from the nearby Conshohocken Bakery. They're also a great value at $7 for a 12-inch roll with 10 ounces of meat or $11 for a 15-inch roll with 15 ounces. "Not too many people ask for extra meat," says Alba.

Customers eat the sandwiches at stiff-backed wooden booths decorated with mirrors or at a Googie-esque curved counter with fans whirring overhead. The sign outside features a cartoon man with his mouth open wide in anticipation of one of Lou's sandwiches. In other words, Lou's is classic Main Street lunch counter circa 1941, the year that Charlie's grandfather, Lou Bondi, first opened the door.

Lou's curvy lunch counter

AKA NICK & LOU'S

Charlie Alba says his grandfather actually began the business with a partner named Nick. But Alba says, "He didn't do anything," and so Lou Bondi bought him out within the first two years. Nevertheless, Alba notes, "Some old-timers still call it Nick and Lou's."

Foot trouble made Bondi abandon early careers as a barber and postman, and when a little ice cream shop became available just down the street from his father's meat market, Bondi snapped it up. Bondi visited Philadelphia frequently to buy clothes and go to the Camac Street steam baths, and Alba believes his grandfather got the idea to serve steak sandwiches from eating them in Philly.

Norristown families have been eating at Lou's for three generations, or just as long as the Bondi family has been serving them. After Bondi died in 1979, his three daughters took over. Since 1994, Lou's has been owned and run by Lou's daughter Margaret Alba and Charlie and his brother, a Johnson & Wales culinary school graduate also named Lou.

An artist's rendition of founder Lou Bondi

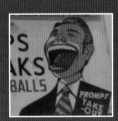

TO GET THERE: From I-76 W, take the Conshohocken exit onto Matsonford Road, which becomes Fayette Street. After crossing the river, take the first left onto Elm Street, which becomes Conshohocken Road. After about three and three-quarter miles, turn left on Ridge Pike, which becomes Main Street, and go a mile. Lou's is located near the corner of Walnut and Main, to the left. By public transportation, take the Regional Rail R6 to Conshohocken and take Bus 97 to Main and Walnut.

OTHER LOCATIONS: Lou's Too, 730 W. Main, Trappe, 610-831-1248, is run by Margaret Alba's other son, Michael, and has a similar menu.

SEATING: For 44, with waitress service

OFF-STREET PARKING: No

ALCOHOL: No

HOURS: 6 a.m. to 8 p.m. Monday through Saturday, 7 a.m. to 3 p.m. Sunday

ROLL: Conshohocken Bakery roll or loaf

MEAT: Sirloin, sliced thin in-house and cooked to order

ONION: Chopped

CHEESE: American (the default), provolone, or imitation Cheez Whiz

GRILL SEASONING: Soybean and olive oil blend

SPECIALTIES: Garlic bread cheesesteak (the roll is slathered with garlic butter and toasted), zep, and the steak zep, which combines Lou's two best sellers into one gut-busting sandwich of cooked steak, salami, tomato, onion, provolone, oil, and oregano

A TASTE EVEN VEGETARIANS CAN'T SHAKE

A vegetarian cheesesteak is "sex without the orgasm," according to Joey Vento of Geno's Steaks. Serious vegetarian chefs view replicating the taste of meat as the lowest form of their art. That could be why bars and steak shops—and not vegetarian places—dominate this list of best places to find vegetarian cheesesteaks in Philly. The standard steak substitute is flavored and cooked wheat gluten, or seitan. This list does not include any rip-off cheesesteaks made only of inexpensive veggies.

For a list of former cheesesteak eater and veggie cheesesteak consultant Jonathan Bagot's latest veggie cheesesteak finds, visit www.yourdaughterstiedupinabrooklynbasement.com.

THE ABBAYE, 637 N. Third St., 215-627-6711. Bar with a beloved fake cheesesteak and cheese sauce and fries accompaniment.

MONK'S, 626 S. 16th St., 215-545-7005. This combo of seitan, onions, mushrooms, and fancy Saint Nectaire cheese is by all accounts delicious. But it's small by steak stand standards, so you'll just have to fill up on beer from Monk's award-winning selection (luckily).

POPE, 1501 E. Passyunk Ave., 215-755-5125. A greasier, slightly better-seasoned version of what Monk is serving (above) from a bar located in the heart of South Philly cheesesteak territory, so they've got chutzpah as well as very fresh rolls.

GIANNA'S GRILLE, 507 S. Sixth St., 215-829-4448. By most estimations, the closest thing to the finely chopped, big and sloppy real thing.

SABRINA'S CAFÉ, 910 Christian St., 215-574-1599. This popular sit-down restaurant's take on the veggie cheesesteak features seitan, cheese, and roasted hot peppers on the same roll used by reigning cheesesteak king John's. *Inquirer* food critic Craig LaBan says it's "as good as a veggie steak can be."

STEVE'S STEAKS, 650 South St., 215-629-9232. Steve's is one of a number of restaurants around town that uses Vegadelphia Foods' Veggie Lean, the Boca Burger of Philly steak substitutes. (see below). This South Street steak shop is a vegetarian's best hope of talking their nonveg friends out of going to the nearby Jim's.

King of Fake Steaks

So just how popular are cheesesteaks in Philadelphia? So popular that the city can support a business devoted to supplying restaurants with a vegetarian faux steak.

Vegadelphia Foods is a sister company to Shipon's Steaks, the pioneering processor of chicken for chicken cheesesteaks. "For years chicken was what people turned to when they wanted a healthier cheesesteak option," says Shipon's Steaks vice president Seth Shipon. "Vegetarian was the natural next step for us."

Vegadelphia's Veggie Lean steak product was actually a 2002 brainstorm of Seth's brother, Garris, then a vegetarian. The wheat-based product has zero trans fats, zero cholesterol, and high protein while mimicking the chew and look of Philly steak meat. Topped with cheese and onions and placed on good Italian bread, "you could fake someone out with it," boasts Shipon's Steaks founder Alvin Shipon, Seth and Garris's dad.

In 2007 People for the Ethical Treatment of Animals (PETA) named the Philadelphia Phillies' Citizens Bank Park the most vegetarian-friendly ballpark in America, largely on the basis of the Veggie Lean cheesesteaks served by concessionaire Rick's Steaks.

Seth Shipon (left) with his dad Alvin, who was initially skeptical about the idea of a veggie cheesesteak

Mama's Pizza

426 BELMONT AVE., BALA CYNWYD,
610-664-4758, WWW.MAMASPIZZERIA.COM

Mama's is probably the only cheesesteak place in America decorated with clown pictures. Paul Castellucci Jr. says his father, Paul, the restaurant's founder, put them up out of the belief that "clowns make people happy." (They certainly would give some of the tattoo-adorned, chain-wearing steak slingers in South Philly a laugh.)

You also don't see too many steak shops where the tables are covered with tablecloths and decorated with fake flowers in single-stem flower vases like at Mama's. The steaks themselves are also different: their meat is

Paul Castellucci Jr. carries on the family tradition – along with a couple of cheesesteak hoagies.

smothered in so big a blend of three secret shredded cheeses as to put a lactose-intolerant person in a coma. And yet on Philly's wealthy suburban Main Line, Mama's is as beloved and respected a cheesesteak institution as Steve's or Dalessandro's are in their neighborhoods.

Many of Mama's idiosyncrasies can be traced to its 1958 start as a pizza and pasta restaurant named after Paul Sr.'s Italian-Albanian mother. Paul Sr.'s wife, Miriam, began making cheesesteaks by customer demand a few years later. At first she used a frying pan, but the cheesesteaks soon became so popular that she and Paul Sr. added a flat-top grill and dropped the pasta from the menu. Because the cheesesteaks were not planned, she used the pizza cheese she had on hand. It makes for

a very cheesy sandwich that Paul Jr. admits is not universally loved. "People are either, 'This is not a cheesesteak' or 'Oh my God, this is the best cheesesteak I've ever had in my life.'"

Its fans are devoted—they are responsible for 70 to 80 percent of all Mama's business and by Paul Jr.'s estimate, 70 percent of them are regulars. You'd almost have to be a regular to know about the cheesesteaks (the sign on the building only says "Mama's Pizza" and the place does no advertising) or to find Mama's. It's hidden behind a tree on a curve of a very windy, heavily trafficked road near Laurel Hill Cemetery (which could come in handy should you misjudge the death-defying turn into or out of Mama's driveway).

Although Paul Jr. added lunch in 1978 to cater to the increased local traffic, Mama's still has quite limited hours compared to most cheesesteak places. Paul Jr. explains that that's because it's still run by family. In fact, a Web poster who once asked a Mama's waitress for the secret behind the cheesesteaks was told the following: "I have been working here for five years, and they trust me with everything, including all the money. But they will not let me cook the steaks. Only family does that."

That, even more than the clown pictures, is probably what makes Mama's customers happy.

Sides and Desserts

WHIZ-DRIZZLED FRIES and local potato chips such as Herr's or Wise are popular sides. You shouldn't have room for dessert, but you might want to buy a **PEANUT CHEW** (née Goldenberg's) or packaged **TASTYKAKE** snack cake for later. Peanut Chews are a locally born and made dark chocolate peanut and molasses candy bar. Tastykake is Philly's equivalent of Hostess, only made with better-quality ingredients. Butterscotch-frosted Krimpets and Kandy Kakes (disk-shaped chocolate-coated candy-cake hybrids filled with peanut butter or vanilla cream) are solid Tastykake choices.

TO GET THERE: From I-76 W, take the Montgomery Drive/West River Drive exit and turn left on Montgomery. After about half a mile, turn right on Belmont and go two and a quarter miles. Mama's Pizza is located just past the overpass.

SEATING: For about 40 in two small but fancily decorated rooms

OFF-STREET PARKING: Yes

ALCOHOL: No

HOURS: 11 a.m. to 2 p.m. Tuesday, until 9 p.m. Wednesday through Saturday

ROLL: Custom-made, about 6 inches wide and 10 inches long

MEAT: Rib-eye, cooked slowly and sliced so thinly that it falls apart on the grill

ONION: Diced and cooked with the meat

CHEESE: Secret blend of three shredded pizza cheeses (and lots of it)

GRILL SEASONING: Vegetable oil blend

SPECIALTIES: The Cordon Bleu, which is a cheesesteak wrapped in Italian ham. "Some people are scared to get it, but then they get stuck on it," says Castellucci. And bread expert and suburban Philly native Peter Reinhart begins his 2003 pizza book, *American Pie,* with nostalgic musings about childhood dinners of Mama's pizza. (See page 156 for Reinhart's recipe for Italian Rolls.)

Pagano's Steaks & Hoagies

7617 OGONTZ AVE., WEST OAK LANE, PHILADELPHIA, 215-549-1646

talians may have been the first to make cheesesteaks, but Greeks have since developed a taste for steaks (as they did earlier for pizza). Prominent Greeks in the cheesesteak business include Demi Kollias of Claymont Steak Shop, Nicholas Karamatsoukas and George Kontodemos of the Original Philadelphia Cheesesteak meat company, and Pagano's owner Alexandro Apsis, former owner of the Explorer's Den, whose 2008 purchase of the landmark Dalessandro's made him a major steak player.

Apsis was making sausage and grinding meat in his father's butcher shop in Greece when he was nine years old. By twelve, he had graduated to the register, which in those days, meant pencil on butcher paper. He says, "I don't know sports because when I was a kid, I was working. But I know meat like a mechanic knows cars."

Three days after arriving in America, the teenage Apsis was employed at a pizza shop, where he worked his way up from prep team to cook to manager to store owner with a rapidity that astonished even himself, given his English. "It was so bad," he admits. The "do you understand?" that punctuates almost every other one of Apsis's perfectly under-standable, if heavily accented, sentences even today is no doubt a vestige of his earlier difficulty.

By the early 1980s, Apsis family members owned six Philly area food businesses, including multiple pizza shops and a supper club. But Apsis says he eventually decided that

Cheesesteak magnate Alexandro Apsis

it would be "easier to do only a couple of things instead of two hundred," and "easier to be the best if you specialize." He decided on steaks in 1998 when distant relative Bill Pagano was ready to retire. Apsis bought Explorer's Den from another relative two years later (but sold it in late 2007 when he got a generous offer from the adjacent La Salle University).

Like Explorer's, Pagano's is a takeout-only stand famous for its large sandwiches. Apsis has maintained that tradition, as well as the shop's thirty-eight-year-old moving neon sign, although he has made some improvements to the interior: a new tile floor, bright yellow and white walls, and, in a bow to the neighborhood and the shop's primarily African American population, framed pictures of black heroes like Martin Luther King Jr. and Joe Frazier rather than Greeks Michael Dukakis, George Stephanopoulous or—given his rising fame on the Philly cheesesteak scene—Apsis himself.

BEEF COWS ARE BORN, BUT MOST CHEESESTEAK MEAT IS MADE (AND HERE'S HOW)

TO GET THERE: From I-76 W, bear right at Roosevelt Expressway/US-1 N. Take the Broad Street/PA-611 Exit and merge onto St. Luke Street. Take the third left onto Broad. After two miles, turn left on Stenton and go half a mile. Bear right on Ogontz and go about a mile and a half. Pagano's Steaks & Hoagies is located between 76th and 77th, to the left.

SEATING: Takeout only

OFF-STREET PARKING: No

ALCOHOL: No

HOURS: 10 a.m. to midnight or 1 a.m. Monday through Saturday

ROLL: Amoroso's

MEAT: Rib-eye, sliced in-house

ONION: Diced and precooked halfway before the steaks

CHEESE: Whiz, American, or provolone, put in the roll and then covered with the hot meat

GRILL SEASONING: 25 percent olive oil, 75 percent vegetable oil blend

The Original Philadelphia Cheesesteak Company is located in a nondescript one-story factory building marked with a vinyl-looking sign—as if the twenty-eight-year-old establishment were a dollar store that might not last the week. Not likely. As the name implies, this is one of Philadelphia's oldest, largest, and most successful producers of meat for cheesesteaks, and its flagship 80,000-square-foot facility on East Hunting Park Avenue in Northeast Philly processes more than 100,000 pounds of meat a day. It also houses the company's administrative office, which looks like any modern office—but smells like a butcher shop.

Everyone has been warned against learning how legislation or sausage is made. Chopped and formed cheesesteak meat is rightly not mentioned in the same breath because in comparison it seems neither very scary nor all that complicated. In part, that could be because the Original Philadelphia's operation is all post-slaughter.

The steak-making process begins with 4-foot tubs and 2 x 3-foot boxes of refrigerated raw boneless beef. Helmeted workers plop these roast-sized pieces on a conveyor belt that carries them to the top of what looks like a giant meat grinder with a funnel-like top, which breaks the roasts down into baseball-sized chunks.

Another conveyor carries these pieces over to a 9 x 5-foot rectangular mixer with big rotary blades, which mixes the meat with water and seasoning. After about ten minutes, the mixture travels down another conveyor and into plastic-lined 4 x 8 x 22-inch metal molding trays. The white-jacketed workers huddle around the trays and pat the meat down in a way that make them look like surgeons performing an operation, but Original Philadelphia Cheesesteak Company vice president and tour guide John Karamatsoukas says that what they're actually doing is getting the air out and sealing the top in more plastic.

The trays are then stacked on pallets between metal sheets until they reach about chest high. Next the pallets are wheeled into a blast freezer set between negative 20 and negative 40 degrees. One to two days later, the pallets are moved to the tempering room, which is a comparatively balmy 26 to 30 degrees. (In order to be cut to the traditional paper-thinness, the meat must be at least somewhat frozen, and it's still frozen when it's sliced in steak shops.)

After the long bricks of red meat are removed from their molds, they are loaded vertically onto what look like large movie projectors but are really slicing machines with rotary buzz saws, which cut the meat into one-ounce slices and automatically intersperse those slices with pieces of waxed paper before they take a final conveyor belt ride into a cardboard box. The boxes are stacked, put on yet more pallets, and stored in another giant freezer for their eventual journey to a steak shop. Karamatsoukas says that for local shops that use his company's products, the time between animal slaughter and the moment when your teeth sinks into that beef can be as short as three weeks.

Peppermill

813 N. CHESTER RD., EAST GOSHEN, 215-692-0100

With a name like Peppermill, you might expect an old inn or tavern with a bartender grilling up steaks behind the bar. Instead this place, with its pine paneling, "country kitchen" draperies, and decoupaged Coke ad decor embodies the phrase "locally patronized family restaurant circa 1970s." It serves what Alice might have given the Brady kids for lunch, if the Bradys had lived in the Philadelphia suburbs instead of California. That means hoagies, pizza, and especially cheesesteaks, which have won a number of local newspaper and magazine awards, *Philadelphia* magazine ones in 2005 and 2008.

The Peppermill's future life as a popular local restaurant nearly ended with a fire in about 1980 because the owner had no insurance. Fortunately a relative who had hit it big in Atlantic City stepped in with a loan, and the Peppermill's destiny as East Goshen's best source of cheesesteaks was fulfilled.

"Fire in the hole!"

The Peppermill's current owner is Rick Welder, a former corporate lawyer with a deliberate manner whose initial forays into the kitchen in 1990 were by his own admission pretty much of a disaster. They include the busy Friday night he was charged with taking the pizzas out of the convection ovens, when one particularly cheesy pizza stuck to the screen and orders began to back up like in the famous *I Love Lucy* candy factory episode. Or the evening, also early on in Welder's reign, when he peered into one of these same ovens, saw "an enormous flame" (really just a normal pilot light), and began screaming, "Fire in the hole! Shut 'er down!"

"Let's just say I learned what I should be involved with, and what I should not," he says dryly. So now Welder stays mainly behind the scenes, counting the proverbial beans and riding herd over the quality of Peppermill food supplies. Here is Welder on the American cheese that is preferred in Delaware County: "Of course I'm concerned about flavor but

Father and son cheesesteak titans Rick (right) and Andrew Welder

also what happens when you subject the cheese to heat. A lot of cheeses become watery. We're looking for something that becomes creamy."

With a customer base of 95 percent regulars, Welder says he will usually "change things only if something is not available." But when the Peppermill's longtime sirloin steak product started exhibiting rubber-band-like pieces of cartilage, a switch had to be made. "Fortunately it was pretty seamless. Nobody seemed to notice," he says with the satisfaction of a fighter pilot recalling a successful mission.

Since spring of 2008, Welder's administrative skills have been complemented by the more hands-on experience his son, Andrew, twenty-nine, acquired by attending Cornell's hotel school and directing the liquor programs for Mario Batali and Lidia Bastianich restaurants in New York City. But don't expect the Peppermill to go BYO with Andrew-suggested microbrew-cheesesteak pairings anytime soon. Rick practically shutters at the suggestion. "We have a pretty large senior citizen clientele and I wouldn't want anyone to be uncomfortable," he says.

TO GET THERE: From I-76 W, take the King of Prussia/West Chester exit and merge onto US-202 S toward West Chester. In about four miles, take the Paoli exit onto West Swedesford Road/PA-252 S. After about two and a half miles, turn right on US-30. Bear left on Paoli Pike. After about five miles, bear left on North Chester Road. Peppermill is located near the corner of East Boot Road and Chester, to the left.

SEATING: Booth and table seating for about 50

OFF-STREET PARKING: Yes

ALCOHOL: Absolutely not

HOURS: 10:30 a.m. to 9 or 10 p.m. Sunday through Thursday, 8 a.m. to 11 p.m. or midnight Fridays and Saturdays

ROLL: Conshohocken Bakery

MEAT: Sirloin, finely chopped

ONION: Precooked, chopped, and thoroughly worked into the meat

CHEESE: White American is the default, although Whiz and provolone are also available.

GRILL SEASONING: Salt and pepper only

SPECIALTIES: Triple Cheesesteak with American, provolone, and mozzarella cheeses; the South of the Border Chicken Cheesesteak, featuring sliced cherry peppers and some other spicy ingredients the Welders won't reveal; and milk shakes

CELEBRITY CUSTOMERS: Baseball great Johnny Bench, "Jackass" Bam Margera, and comedienne Joan Rivers (at least, according to her lackeys who pick up her orders from the nearby QVC)

Philip's

2234 W. PASSYUNK AVE., SOUTH
PHILADELPHIA, 215-755-4820

The tourists have spoiled Pat's, goes one familiar local cheesesteak complaint. What incentive would anyone have to keep the quality high when hours-long lines of tourists are guaranteed no matter what you serve?

What's a local who wants a quick and tasty lunch rather than a pilgrimage to a junk food shrine to do? Many in-the-knowsters drive five minutes west on Passyunk into deep South Philadelphia to Philip's. The circa 1983 shop has the classic ordering window design and traffic island setting and the Big Cheesesteak Triangle's convenient 24/7 schedule. It's as clean as Geno's but is free of Geno's politics. Says morning grill man Gregory Caccauo, "We don't care what language you speak. You can talk gibberish—a lot of our customers do—we'll take the time to explain things to you."

This is not to say that Philip's never has a line. It does, especially on Friday and Saturday nights and weekday midafternoons, when the nearby GAMP magnet school lets out. But the lines are made up almost entirely of local regulars. The reason becomes obvious if you show up at nine in the morning, when the sparkling white and stainless steel interior is alive with preparations: onions being diced, logs of rib-eye steak being sliced, and big trays of just-cut long hot peppers in big metal pans waiting for the hams to come out of the oven. (Yes, they roast their own pork too.) As Caccauo,

manager Santo, and meat slicer Tommy work, people walk in and out with fresh deliveries or fresh talk. "When a girl asks you where the beach is, you point like this," says one heavily tattooed kitchen visitor with a grin while talking about the Shore, angling his arm in a way to showcase his pectorals.

There are no celebrity photos and no souvenir T-shirts—Philip's is the real deal, including one aspect that could keep the tourists away. Namesake and founder Philip Narducci is an alleged mobster currently serving a multi-decades federal prison sentence for racketeering offenses, or, as Santo low-keys it, "He got in trouble and is away."

TO GET THERE: From I-76 E, take the Passyunk Avenue/Oregon Avenue exit. Turn left on Passyunk and go about a quarter of a mile. Philip's is located at the intersection of Passyunk and Croskey, to the right. By public transportation, take Bus 7 to Passyunk and 23rd, then walk east on Passyunk.

SEATING: No, but there is a metal counter under the awning for stand-up eating

OFF-STREET PARKING: Yes, right across the street

ALCOHOL: No

HOURS: 24/7, except major holidays

ROLL: D'Ambrosio's loaves cut into 10-inch rolls

MEAT: Slabs of freshly cut rib-eye

ONION: Diced

CHEESE: Whiz, ladled from a steel canister that warms on the side of the grill. American and provolone are other options.

GRILL SEASONING: Oil blend

SPECIALTIES: Milano's-style pizza steaks (see page 104) and sausage sandwiches. Wash it all down with a water ice from the equally authentic-looking (but unaffiliated) Dati stand across the street.

STORY: Two firebombs were thrown into the shop late one night in November 1985. Employees escaped through the takeout windows, but the bombs were duds and nothing but the speed of sandwich service was hurt.

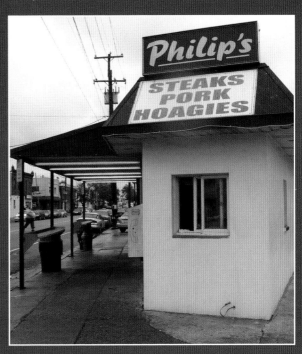

IT'S A SMALL (STEAK) WORLD

- Pat's King of Steaks once employed Tim De Salis of Talk of the Town and Samuel Sherman of Chink's
- Geno's once employed Tim De Salis of Talk of the Town
- A Dalessandro's aunt worked at both Dalessandro's and Chubby's
- One of the founders of Chubby's once worked at Pudge's
- Jim's Steaks co-owner Abner Silver opened Abner's. Jim's Steaks founder Millie Pearlingi was a cousin of Larry's Steaks founder Larry Marroney.
- Big John's employee Bart Brown went on to start Ishkabbibble's.
- Domenic Mark Spataro of Spataro's is the cousin of Chick's Deli co-owner Tony Della Monica.

Pudge's

1530 DEKALB PIKE (ROUTE 202), BLUE BELL, 610-277-1717, WWW.PUDGESSTEAKS.COM

Pudge's name calls attention to the idea that cheesesteaks are bad for you. In this case, the idea is probably accurate. The large sandwich is twenty inches long and so overstuffed that new customers who can finish it on-site get half off the price. Pudge's will even put different toppings on different halves of the sandwich, pizza-maker-style, to accommodate sharers.

The shop's name doesn't actually refer to the size of the sandwiches but to founder Frank Carbone, who acquired the nickname as a pudgy child. Pudge and his sister took over their mom's Germantown, Philadelphia, neighborhood sandwich shop in the 1960s, but a dramatic robbery where Pudge, his wife, and his sister were lined up with guns to their heads sent them running to the burbs.

In 1970 the tidy little luncheonette landed in a tiny strip mall on Route 202 in Blue Bell, where Pudge ruled with an iron spatula. He had one nephew fresh-slicing hoagie meats in the wee hours. And woe to any employee who would mix the cheese into the meat on the cheesesteak so thoroughly that the customer could no longer see that it had cheese in it, his wife, Mary Ann Carbone, recalls.

Sadly, Pudge died of a heart attack (his third) in October 2000. But his daughter Barbara and son-in-law Michael Williams carry on with Pudge-like quality standards, judging from their 2005 *Philadelphia* magazine Best Cheesesteak suburban nod.

Barbara and Michael Williams

The shop's chef logo is from a customer's cartoon sketch of Pudge.

TO GET THERE: From I-76 W, take the Plymouth Meeting exit and merge onto I-476 N. After three and a half miles, take the Germantown Pike-East/Plymouth Meeting exit onto Chemical Road. Turn left at West Germantown Pike. After about three and a quarter miles, turn right onto DeKalb Pike/US-202. Pudge's is located a mile down DeKalb Pike, to the right.

OTHER LOCATIONS: Pudge's II, 2117 W. Main St., Norristown, 610-630-9180 (though it's no longer in the family)

SEATING: For about 25 at simple dark wood tables, with waitress service

OFF-STREET PARKING: Yes

ALCOHOL: No

HOURS: Noon to 8 or 8:30 p.m. Tuesday through Saturday

ROLL: Conshohocken Bakery

MEAT: Old Philly Style brand beef sandwich steak

ONION: Chopped and precooked

CHEESE: Thick-sliced American or a Cheez Whiz knockoff

GRILL SEASONING: No

SPECIALTIES: Homemade Italian wedding soup, hot peppers, and coleslaw

STORY: Pudge's daughter Barbara swore off red meat of all kinds after seeing the steak meat being sliced in her dad's shop at age twelve.

Rick's Steaks

CENTER CITY, PHILADELPHIA
WWW.RICKSSTEAKS.COM

Frank Olivieri Sr. and Jr. may be the most famous descendants of Pat Olivieri in the cheesesteak business, but they're not the only ones. Pat's grandson and Frank Sr's nephew, Rick Olivieri, has also been standing behind a grill for more than a quarter century.

When Pat Olivieri retired to California in the mid-1960s, his brother, Harry, got the Ninth Street stand and Pat's son, Herb, got Pat's Dauphin Street restaurants and the right to open stands under the Pat's name everywhere but within three and a half miles of Ninth Street. That's why the stand he opened in the Reading Terminal Market in 1982 was called Olivieri Prince of Steaks.

Rick worked his dad's shops from age fourteen. "It was not even like a job to me. I loved it—talking to customers, making them happy," Rick recalls in an interview at his shop, which he interrupts several times to chat or exchange hugs with customers. That might make Rick seem primarily like a people person, but he also has the keen head for business that his dad lacked, judging from Herb's lack of success.

Time was really Herb's problem, Rick explains: "He was deputy attorney general at the time—and this is not a turnkey business. If somebody puts just a slice or two of extra meat, you can be giving away a couple of one hundred sandwiches in one day." (See opposite page and 27 for more on Herb and Olivieri family politics.) In any case, Rick took over his dad's old spot at the Reading Terminal Market in 1995, renaming it Rick's Steaks.

Reading Terminal Market was in disrepair when the Olivieris first got there. But by the time Rick's opened, a refurbished Market was part of Philadelphia's sparkling new convention center, and the downtown office workers and regional rail commuters who had always patronized the stand were supplemented by conventiongoers in search of their first cheesesteak.

Rick on wrapping detail

The sandwich they got was slab-style like Pat's. Rick also likes Cheez Whiz, although as at Pat's, other cheeses are available. The main differences are the more expensive and, Rick believes, more flavorful chuck-eye meat he uses and cooks on the grill with water instead of oil.

Rick became head of the Market's union-like Merchants Association about the same time as market management was introducing new leases, which he helped his fellow shopkeepers fight. So when Rick's own lease came up, management said they assumed he would not want to renew and started talking with Tony Luke about taking Rick's place.

The usual hue and cry that arises anytime a longtime merchant is asked to leave the Market was compounded in this case by Rick's cheesesteak pedigree. (For more on Reading Terminal Market, see page 113.) For almost two years, the local media chronicled the Rick lease story, including fellow merchants' cancellation of the annual Amish Festival in protest, a petition drive that yielded more than three thousand signatures, and the legal battle that resulted in Rick's agreeing to leave by fall 2008.

As of this writing, Rick's Steaks is still looking for a new home, most likely in Center City Philly. But two things are certain: 1. Rick will be making steaks somewhere and 2. all the publicity should make him very easy to find.

HIS STEAK KINGDOM FOR A SPOT ON THE CITY COUNCIL

In a 1951 *Philadelphia Inquirer* article, Pat Olivieri spoke of someday running the Pat's Steaks business with his only son, Herb. "It'll be great. Me and the boy—together," he hoped aloud.

It was not to be. The son of the inventor of Philadelphia's iconic sandwich ended up being associated instead with a quite different city icon: City Hall's thirty-seven-foot-tall sculpture of Philadelphia founder William Penn.

Herb's education may have been partly responsible. Degrees from Friends Select, Wharton, and University of Pennsylvania Law would appear to be better preparation for filing lawsuits and drafting legislation than making steaks. And in fact, Herb Olivieri was an attorney who staged a number of unsuccessful campaigns for the Philadelphia city council before becoming Pennsylvania deputy attorney general in 1979. Herb was still in that office when he decided to exploit the franchise rights he had acquired after his father's 1970 death, and so it was a royalty arrangement with other people running the company. That Pat's International Ltd. chain ended in bankruptcy, and Herb successfully sued the company to get the Pat's name back.

Herb himself was at the helm of his second attempt to franchise Pat's in 1987—not that it turned out that much better. A highlight was the April 27, 1989, opening of a Pat's Steaks in Manhattan attended by a fully feathered Hegeman String Band, ex-Phillie Larry Christenson, and a live, hay-munching version of the Angus steer used to make the sandwiches. But that shop only lasted eighteen months. And financial and legal troubles plagued the other shops he opened.

But the late 1980s was also when Herb engineered his biggest success: a drive to raise money to renovate City Hall's giant William Penn before the city's 1987 Constitution bicentennial celebration. That—and not cheesesteaks—is what Herb's 1998 *Philadelphia Inquirer* obituary focused on.

OTHER LOCATION: Citizens Bank Park, 1 Citizens Bank Way, 215-463-1000

ROLL: Liscio's

MEAT: Chuck-eye, sliced at the stand and cooked to order in slabs

ONION: Chopped, precooked, and placed on the roll with the meat

CHEESE: Whiz, American, provolone, or mozzarella, placed on the bread and topped with the meat

GRILL SEASONING: Water only

SPECIALTIES: Veggie steaks made with Vegadelphia's Veggie Lean (see page 90)

CHEESESTEAK MENU DECODER

PIZZA CHEESESTEAK: Standard cheesesteak (cheese and beef) with pizza or marinara sauce. Mozzarella or provolone is usually better on this than American or Whiz. A variation sometimes called old-fashioned pizza, old-fashioned, or pizza Milano (after the South Philly steak shop that invented it in the early 1950s) is instead made with grilled fresh tomato and Italian spices.

PEPPER CHEESESTEAK: Standard cheesesteak with grilled chopped hot, sweet, or bell peppers. Note that this is a variation. That the standard cheesesteak contains bell peppers is probably outlanders' most common misconception. If this is what you want, this is what you'll need to order.

CHEESESTEAK HOAGIE: Standard cheesesteak with lettuce, tomatoes, raw onions, and sometimes mayo with contrasting hot and cold, soft and crisp textures. (This is not simply a cheesesteak served in the standard hoagie roll, as some tourists assume.)

MUSHROOM CHEESESTEAK: Standard cheesesteak with cut-up cooked mushrooms.

STEAK: A thin-sliced steak (not a T-bone or a Porterhouse) with no cheese. For about twenty years this was the only way the sandwiches were sold. It's why Philly old-timers call the places that make them "steak shops," not cheesesteak joints.

CHICKEN CHEESESTEAK: A cheesesteak with thinly sliced chicken meat instead of (and not in addition to) thinly sliced beef or, less commonly, chopped-up cubes of chicken meat. A sandwich made with chicken tenders or breast meat technically should not be called a cheesesteak, although it sometimes is. Chicken steak varieties usually mimic the beef, with a few exceptions (the Buffalo chicken cheesesteak with wing sauce and blue cheese being among the most notable). See page 71 for the chicken cheesesteak's origins.

ACCEPTABLE/COMMON CONDIMENTS: Options include peppers of all kinds, but especially hot cherry peppers, long hot peppers, roasted red peppers, and dried chili peppers; hot pepper relish; hot sauce; ketchup; pepperoni; bacon; and dill or sweet pickles (if you must). Many of these come gratis at the condiments bar; others you must ask and pay for separately. Note that this list does not include mustard or mayo, and that a really good steak probably won't need any condiments.

Shank's & Evelyn's

932 S. 10TH ST., BELLA VISTA, SOUTH PHILADELPHIA, 215-629-1093

On the early spring day I last visited Shank's and Evelyn's, a man had set up a temporary tackle shop on the sidewalk next door. As I checked out the wares, two cops walked into the luncheonette—only to come back out a moment later with someone they began questioning in front of the minnow nets.

This, my friends, is South Philadelphia, and Shank's and Evelyn's is a quintessential South Philly luncheonette. Long famed for slow-roasted roast beef and roast pork served on Italian bread, sales of these old favorites are gradually being overtaken by chicken cutlet and steak sandwiches crafted with the same quality standards. The cheesesteaks, for instance, are made with top round that is sliced by hand and grilled to order—and is never chopped. Business namesake and cofounder Evelyn Perri, catlike and sophisticated in an all-black outfit, looks pained at the suggestion. "Chopping would take all the juice out of it," she protests.

This building has been the lone official business in a row of residential row houses for as long as anyone can remember. In the early 1950s, it was an auto parts store owned by Perri's father-in-law, then a kids arcade with a small food concession run by his son, Evelyn's late husband, Frank, also known as "Shank." (Frank got the Shank nickname from a little brother who couldn't pronounce his *F*s.) A remodeler trying to drum up more work pushed the Perris deeper into the food business. Evelyn recalls, "He was working on the bathroom in our apartment upstairs and suggested we let him lengthen the lunch counter." So they did, expanding the counter to accommodate a whopping eight stools and expanding the menu along with it.

At first, Evelyn was the one making the family Italian specialties for the public; then Shank and his son Frank took over, and now it's daughter Pamela. The waitstaff is also mainly family who know each other too well and have worked together too long to be bothered with niceties when talking to one another. Let's just say they're not above yelling in front of customers. "Some of the newer people take it the wrong way," Evelyn concedes. "Sure, we say things sometimes— but then it blows right over."

Despite or maybe because of this atmosphere, Shank's and Evelyn's has long been a favorite of local Italian politicians (who feel right at home) and visiting actors and musicians (known for staging their own dramatics). Signed souvenirs of visits by Connie Francis, Patty Duke, Mario Lanza, and Bill Cosby decorate Shank's and Evelyn's right wall.

But Evelyn admits that "a lot of our old regulars have died or can't eat this kind of food anymore." Evelyn herself stopped eating meat when her husband got sick fifteen years ago. She says, "I was running from here to the hospital and just grabbing quick stuff like salads. I just kind of lost my taste for it."

Evelyn communes with some regulars.

TO GET THERE: From I-76 E, bear left onto I-676 E/Vine Street Expressway. Take the Eighth Street exit and turn right on Eighth. After about three-quarters of a mile, turn right on Catharine Street. Go about a quarter of a mile on Catharine, then turn left on Tenth. Shank's and Evelyn's is located at the intersection of Tenth and Hall, to the right. Public transportation options include Bus 23 (down 12th Street to Christian) or Bus 47 (down Eighth Street to Christian).

SEATING: 6 tables and 8 stools at the counter

OFF-STREET PARKING: No

ALCOHOL: No

HOURS: 7:30 a.m. to 4 p.m. Monday through Saturday

ROLL: Liscio's 24-inch loaf, cut in half

MEAT: Top round, hand-sliced

ONION: Chopped and cooked with the steak (in part because Evelyn doesn't want to take the smell of onions home)

CHEESE: American or provolone

GRILL SEASONING: Oil blend

SPECIALTIES: Roast beef, roast pork, and chicken cutlet sandwiches; homemade soups; and the Bellybuster Giambitta six-egg omelet

Silvio's

100 N. YORK RD., HATBORO,
215-674-8843

Some say the secret to a great cheesesteak is the bread. Those people should go to Silvio's Deli, where every roll is made on the premises fresh every morning.

The business actually started out as a bakery owned by Frank Vechione in the early 1980s. Vechione began putting meat on the bread not too long before Silvio and Susan Frate took over, changed the name, and moved to a building across the street.

The space the public sees is essentially an enclosed deli counter, decorated on the nonbakery side with sandwich awards, Philly sports photos, and Italian food posters, along with a snapshot of the late Silvio. Nowadays his mustachioed son Steven mans the cash register, and five women make the sandwiches to the sound of a constantly jangling phone.

The cheesesteaks are made with an eclectic blend of top round beef, Cooper cheese, and sliced (not diced) Bermuda onion. But Steven Frate lists all these ingredients almost dismissively. "It's the bread that makes the difference between our cheesesteaks and everyone else's," he says. "A machine can not make it. There are too many variables. When it's real hot out, you've got to make the bread with cold water. If it's cold, you've got to wait around for it to warm up."

So important is the bread to Frate's business that when it runs out, the shop closes.

TO GET THERE: From I-95 N, take the Woodhaven Road exit and merge onto PA-63 W/Woodhaven Road. After passing the Roosevelt Boulevard intersection, turn left onto Evans Street, then take the first right onto Byberry Road. Follow Byberry for about seven and a quarter miles, then turn right on York. Silvio's Deli is located near the intersection of York and Montgomery, to the right. By public transportation, take Regional Rail R2 to Hatboro Station, walk west to York, and then about a quarter of a mile northeast up York. Or take the Broad Street subway line to Olney Station and take Bus 22, which stops at York and Montgomery.

SEATING: One picnic table out front

OFF-STREET PARKING: Yes

ALCOHOL: No

HOURS: 9 a.m. to 6 or 7 p.m. Monday through Friday, until 4 p.m. Saturday (or until the bread runs out)

ROLL: The shop makes its own.

MEAT: Top round, thin-sliced and chopped

ONION: Bermuda, sliced and cooked with the meat

CHEESE: Cooper, a sharp white American-style cheese

GRILL SEASONING: Salt, pepper, and vegetable oil

SPECIALTIES: Homemade meatballs, homemade chicken salad, and award-winning hoagies

CELEBRITY STORY: The shop wall features a picture of Marilyn Monroe with Bob Faulkner, a customer who posed for it long before he started coming to Silvio's (but who was bothered by Silvio's lack of celebrity snaps).

Sonny's Famous Steaks

228 MARKET ST., OLD CITY,
PHILADELPHIA, 215-629-5760,
WWW.SONNYSFAMOUSSTEAKS.COM

If Kevin Bagby wasn't doing what he does now, he probably could get a job as a Cheez Whiz salesman. In a sense, that *is* his job. As manager of a cheesesteak restaurant on the edge of Philadelphia's tourist and club districts, Bagby, twenty-seven, spends a huge part of his workday tutoring visitors in Philadelphia's cheesesteak culture, including the hard-to-swallow news that Whiz is the way to go. Tradition is only part of his argument. He also thinks that Cheez Whiz is the only cheese strong enough to hold its own tastewise against the flavorful rib-eye Sonny's uses. And indeed, Sonny's won *Philadelphia* magazine's Best of Philly award its first year in business and praise from *Philadelphia Inquirer* restaurant critic Craig LaBan for its "superbly tender, flavorful sandwich."

Walk across Sonny's creaking wood floor to the point where you can see Sonny's stainless steel open kitchen and simple menu, and it's easy to believe the place dates back to Pat and Jim days. But Sonny's is actually only a nine-year-old re-creation of an old cheesesteak stand in a former Norelco store. In other words, it's about as close to the real thing as Cheez Whiz is to 100 percent natural cheese.

Among other things, there is no Sonny. Sonny's owners, Stuart and Ellen Mogell, just came up with that name because they thought it sounded Italian in a way "Stuart and Ellen" didn't. And while manager Bagby likes to give his customers a taste of the traditional cheesesteak shop hard time, it's more of the kidding kind. Like sometimes when it's not busy and people don't order "wit" the proper terminology, Bagby will kiddingly tell them to get to the back of the nonexistent line.

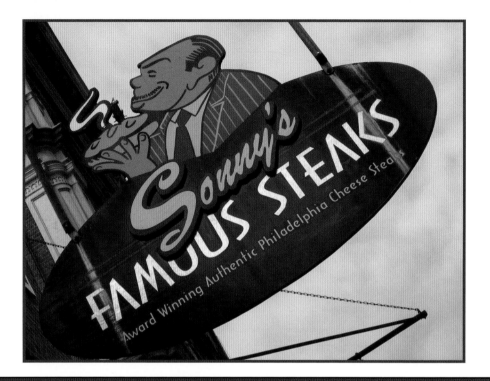

TO GET THERE: From I-76 E, bear left onto I-676 E/Vine Street Expressway. Take the Eighth Street exit and turn right on Eighth. After about half a mile, turn left onto Market. Go half a mile. Sonny's Famous Steaks is located between Banks and Strawberry, to the right. By public transportation, Sonny's is a block from the Second Street stop on the Market-Frankford subway line and a ten-minute walk down Market Street from the Market East Regional Rail Station.

SEATING: For 50, including a couple of outside tables in nice weather

OFF-STREET PARKING: No

ALCOHOL: No

HOURS: 11 a.m. to 10 p.m. Sunday through Thursday, until 3 a.m. Friday and Saturday

ROLL: Amoroso's loaves, cut

MEAT: Rib-eye, sliced on-premises and served slab-style

ONION: Spanish, diced, cooked in batches, and held to the side of the grill

CHEESE: Whiz slathered on the roll; slices of American or provolone melted on the meat if you insist (Bagby thinks they're too mild)

GRILL SEASONING: Nothing added. Bagby thinks the fat from nicely marbled meat is flavorful enough.

SPECIALTIES: Semi-obscene "Bite Me" Sonny's cheese-steak T-shirts

Spataro's

1136 ARCH ST., CENTER CITY, PHILADELPHIA, 215-925-6833, WWW.READINGTERMINALMARKET.ORG

Rick's may be the most famous cheesesteak place ever to grace Philly's famous Reading Terminal Market (in part because of its owner's royal pedigree as the grandson of cheesesteak's inventor, in part because of his well-publicized ouster), but it's not the only one. Or the only good one. Since fall 2006, Spataro's sandwich stand has been grilling up cheesesteaks that are almost exact replicas of the *Philadelphia* magazine award-winners at Cherry Hill's Chick's Deli (see page 40). They're just the latest offering from a man who has been working in Reading Terminal Market since 1930, or longer than any other current Market merchant.

Domenic Charles Spataro was eleven years old when he began helping out at William Troelsch's buttermilk stand. In 1947 he took over a competitive business that ran the forty-foot length of what is now Godshall's Poultry and Terraylyn soaps combined. Spataro's old "Drink Buttermilk and Live Forever" sign still hangs above the soap stand.

In those days, tea sandwiches and gingerbread were mere accompaniments to the thick health elixir that he ladled from metal dairy cans that sat on ice-lined counter barrels. On late afternoons, Main Line housewives would stop to refuel from their shopping while their chauffeurs stood nearby, holding their bags. But eventually sandwiches took over, including the FDR-era cream cheese and olive, liverwurst and onion, and oregano and tomato, all of which are still offered.

Buttermilk came off the menu after the cholesterol scare of the 1980s. Spataro's son and business partner, Domenic Mark Spataro, was behind such menu updates as hoagies (in the late 1980s) and cheesesteaks, which came with their 2006 move to a larger Market stand and are now their best seller. That could be because Domenic Mark and Chick's Deli co-owner Tony Della Monica are cousins, and Spataro's is making its cheesesteaks with all the same ingredients and in exactly the same way.

Although younger employees have now taken over the high-pressure sandwich-making duties, Domenic Charles, ninety-two, still works at the stand every day, fueled by years of buttermilk drinking that, if it hasn't made him immortal, has gotten him darn close.

The two Domenics

TO GET THERE: From I-76 E, bear left onto I-676 E/Vine Street Expressway. Take the Broad Street/Central Philadelphia exit onto Vine Street. Go half a mile, then turn right onto 12th. Reading Terminal Market is just past the Pennsylvania Convention Center, to the left. Public transportation options include Regional Rail (exit at Market East Station and follow the signs for the Convention Center), subway lines (take the Market-Frankford subway line to the 13th Street stop or the Broad Street subway line to the City Hall stop), or buses (Bus 33 to 13th and Market or Bus 48 to Market East Station).

SEATING: In adjacent open seating areas of the Market

OFF-STREET PARKING: Discounted parking in a garage across the street with Market purchase

ALCOHOL: No

HOURS: 8 a.m. to 4 p.m. Monday through Saturday

ROLL: Liscio's

MEAT: Trade secret, chopped fine on the grill

ONION: Spanish onions sliced into half moons and cooked on the grill along with the meat

CHEESE: White American or provolone melted on the meat

GRILL SEASONING: None

SPECIALTIES: Cream cheese and olive, liverwurst and onion, and oregano and tomato sandwiches

ALL ABOARD FOR LOCAL EATS

Those visiting Spataro's should plan some extra time to explore its Reading Terminal Market home. For more than a hundred years, this 100 percent local stew of eighty stalls has been the single best place to find and enjoy Philadelphia food favorites like cheesesteaks, hoagies, and pretzels as well as a favorite source of fresh meats, fish, produce, and ethnic and specialty foods for Center City's large residential population.

Since the early 1990s, when the Reading train shed became the grand hall of the Pennsylvania Convention Center, the Market has also become one of the city's most popular destinations for tourists—at least for tourists not prone to sensory overload. At times it seems as if the entire city is crammed into this one block-long building. But the common love of the place generally quells conflicts unless the threat is from an outside force—such as when management asks a longtime merchant to leave (see page 103.)

In addition to Spataro's, Market must-tastes include DiNic's roast pork (see page 81), Delilah's Oprah-recommended mac and cheese, Bassetts' indulgent and historic ice cream (try the dulce de leche–like butterscotch vanilla) and, from the Amish corner, Fisher's freshly made pretzels and the Dutch Eating Place's scrapple (don't ask). Go on your own or tour the Market on one of my twice-a-week Taste of Philly food history walking tours. But definitely go.

Reading Terminal Market, 1136 Arch St., Philadelphia, 215-922-2317, www.readingterminalmarket.org

Steaks on South

308 SOUTH ST., 215-922-7880,
WWW.STEAKSONSOUTH.COM

South Street is Philadelphia's boardwalk—the street that tourists stroll all night and much of the day. Like most of the other business owners on the street, there's nothing Patrick Dougherty likes less than a rainy day. But unlike others, Dougherty loves a late-afternoon thundershower because it means all those people lined up outside half a block away at Jim's will come running for shelter and a cheesesteak in his shop. And though he refuses to bad-mouth anyone else's food, facts are facts. "Once they try my steak," Dougherty claims, "they never go back."

Dougherty spent most of his life in the bar business in Philadelphia. He helped open the Dicken's Inn and later owned the Artful Dodger. "But you can't own a bar if you have a family," Dougherty says. So the year he got married, Dougherty gave up the Artful Dodger, drinking, smoking—everything except fat and cholesterol, fortunately for his future career as a cheesesteak purveyor.

"This is a new kind of cheesesteak place—*clean,*" he declares before proudly displaying the—yes, it's quite clean, and spacious too—first-floor bathroom and open grill. Dougherty is equally open about other aspects of the business. Neither Dickens nor the Artful Dodger had cheesesteaks on the menu, so Dougherty did his research. He still has the four-year-old scraps of paper detailing the length, exact weight, and prices of cheesesteaks sold by his most immediate competitors. He uses Liscio's rolls, real Cheez Whiz, and steer loin for his standard cheesesteak. "I could get something for thirty cents less a pound," Dougherty says, "but it has more fat so it shrinks and you end up having to use more meat. That's just stupid. You gotta buy the right stuff."

Instead of the standard signed celebrity snaps, Steaks on South's walls feature poster-size reproductions of

SOS's Patrick Dougherty

Dougherty's wife's arty photographs of South Street. It must be hard getting celebrities to go to SOS with Jim's being so close and well known, but Dougherty says that's not the reason. "I love the excitement of the street and I want to celebrate it," he explains.

That excitement comes at a price, namely, a rent among the highest of any place in Center City. This old Food Tech restaurant space is not for newcomers or people who don't know how to lure people in. Toward that end, in summer 2008 Dougherty started running a van from the Independence Visitor Center to his shop on weekends. (For $20 tourists get a historically narrated ride to South Street and an SOS cheesesteak lunch.)

Dougherty interrupts his own discussion about the van to run out into the street to greet a passing tourist duck boat driver—yet another tactic in his campaign to convince people that Jim's is not the only good cheesesteak place on South Street.

SOS Steaks On South

Feel free to order in any language.

We will gladly serve you, with brotherly love!

TO GET THERE: From I-76 E, take the South Street exit. Turn left at South Street and go about two and a quarter miles. Steaks on South is located between Orianna and Third, to the right. By public transportation from Center City, take Bus 32 and get off at Lombard and South or take Bus 33 to Market and Fourth and walk about three-quarters of a mile south down Fourth.

SEATING: Tables and counter seating for up to 50

OFF-STREET PARKING: No

ALCOHOL: No

HOURS: 10:30 a.m. to 10 p.m. Sunday through Thursday, until 4 a.m. Friday and Saturday

ROLL: Liscio's 12-inch roll

MEAT: Drexel Foods steer beef loin in regular sandwiches; chargrilled rib-eye available for an 85-cent surcharge

ONION: Chopped into 1.5-inch pieces and sautéed ahead in olive oil

CHEESE: American, provolone, and real Whiz

GRILL SEASONING: None

SPECIALTIES: Old Bay–seasoned fries, roast pork from Esposito's in the Italian Market, and chicken steaks made from cubed chicken breast

Steve's Prince of Steaks

7200 BUSTLETON AVE., OXFORD CIRCLE,
PHILADELPHIA, 215-338-0985,
WWW.STEVESPRINCEOFSTEAKS.COM

The largest concentration of stand alone steak places outside of South Philadelphia is in Northeast Philadelphia. Steve's Prince of Steaks is one big reason. Mr. V's is owned by a former Steve's manager. Frusco's is owned by Mr. V's ex-wife. Even now, so many people come in and hang out at Steve's to try to figure out how it's done that Steve Iliescu, fifty-nine, and his workers have a word for them: *clockers* ("because they're taking note of everything you do," as carefully as a timekeeper at a race). Not that Iliescu minds all that much. "The greatest flattery is if they copy you," he reasons. The other possible explanation for his magnanimousness? "Clocking" is the way *he* got in.

In the 1970s Steve Iliescu was a car mechanic with a Getty dealership and a love of cheesesteaks fed by biweekly runs to Pat's. But by 1980, with the rise of self-service gas stations and gas station mini-marts foretelling the end of true service stations, he decided to make his cheesesteak passion his business. "I did my homework," he says, going to all the important stands, including Chink's, Jim's, and Geno's, although Steve's own first stand, a squat building tacked onto the end of a block of row houses a block from the Roosevelt Mall, had the efficient ordering counter layout of his first cheesesteak love and inspiration, Pat's. He called his business Steve's Prince of Steaks both in deference to Pat's "King of Steaks," the inventor, but also to proclaim himself successor. Or as Iliescu puts it in one of his high-speed raps (a hit with his teenage employees), "Our steaks are worthy of renown, which is why we wear a crown. Don't make a mistake, and be fooled by a fake. There's only one true Prince of Steaks."

Such recognition wasn't a birthright and didn't happen overnight. Iliescu didn't get his first *Philadelphia* magazine Best Cheesesteak award until 1992, and it was fifteen years before he won it again. Judges and ordinary eaters praise his unique melted white American cheese sauce and rolls baked from the old Vilotti company recipe. Iliescu won't say who's making the rolls for him or reveal the type of oil he uses on his grill. "Put that in your book and everyone will copy," he protests. And he should know.

Prince Steve

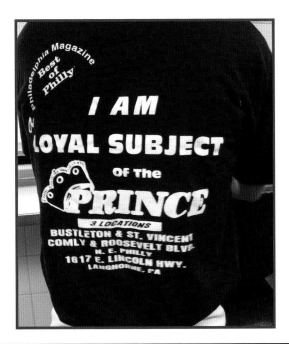

TO GET THERE: From, I-95 N, take the Bridge Street exit. Turn left at the bottom of the exit onto Aramingo, which becomes Harbison. Cross Frankford and Roosevelt, then turn right on Bustleton. Steve's Prince of Steaks is located about half a mile up on the left, near the intersection of St. Vincent and Bustleton. By public transportation, take the Market-Frankford subway line to Frankford Terminal, then take Bus 58 (down Bustleton to St. Vincent Street).

OTHER LOCATIONS: 2711 Comly Rd., Far Northeast, Philadelphia; 1617 E. Lincoln Highway, Langhorne

SEATING: Counter seating for 10

OFF-STREET PARKING: No

ALCOHOL: No

HOURS: 11 a.m. to 11 or 12 p.m. Sunday to Thursday, until 3 a.m. Friday and Saturday

ROLL: Italian torpedoes from a Vilotti company recipe, cut into two 12-inch pieces

MEAT: Rib-eye, sliced fresh throughout the day, unchopped in the Northeast tradition

ONION: Chopped and cooked in small batches throughout the day

CHEESE: Many choices, including mozzarella and American slices, Whiz, Steve's signature white American sauce (liberally applied, although not all that strong tasting), and a sauce combining Whiz and white American

GRILL SEASONING: Oil, but they won't say what kind

SPECIALTIES: White-cheese-sauce-bathed fries

Talk of the Town

3020 S. BROAD ST., SOUTH PHILADELPHIA, 215-551-7277, WWW.SOUTHPHILLY-CHEESESTEAKS.COM

There's hardly a steak shop in Philly without the word *famous* or *best* attached to its name or advertising. It takes another level of hubris or at least hopefulness to call a brand-new business Talk of the Town as Bill D'Ambrosia did in 1997. Twelve years later, this shop is still not talked about with anywhere near the frequency of Pat's or Geno's, but the shop has picked up important endorsements by www.cheesesteaktown.com, Glen Macnow, and Philadelphia Eagles quarterback Donovan McNabb (who personally picks up his chicken cheesesteak hoagies).

Talk of the Town literally arose from the ashes of an old Dairy Queen that burnt down in the late 1980s. Beneath the spiffy new black-and-white color scheme, aluminum seating, and pictures of sports heros lurks the old Blizzard ordering window and enclosed porch. The shop is located in the armpit of I-76 near the stadiums, and many customers are sports fans who are too cheap, impatient, or, manager Tim De Salis prefers to believe, discriminating to buy steaks at the concession stands.

De Salis has been making steaks since he was fifteen, including lengthy stints at Pat's and Geno's, where he says he learned by negative example to cook the food to order and to buy top-quality meat—not just rib-eye but the much more expensive steer kind .

Most of the sports photos that ring the walls and cover the ceiling are unsigned: D'Ambrosia's son, Bill Jr., says he doesn't ask for autographs for fear of making the place a target for break-ins (although the neighborhood doesn't really seem *that* bad). When asked for names of players who've been there besides McNabb, he mentions Aaron Rowand and Bobby Abreu, ex-Phillies who can now only longingly talk about the great steaks at Talk of the Town.

Baseball players A.J. Pierzynski (left) and Aaron Rowand with Talk of the Town's Bill D'Ambrosia Jr.

TALK OF THE LITERARY CROWD

Many cheesesteak shops get travel guide mentions, but Talk of the Town is probably the only one featured in a serious sociological tome. The shop gets several paragraphs in Bruce Buschel's 2007 *Walking Broad* (Simon & Schuster), a snapshot of Philadelphia as viewed via a walk up Broad Street. Talk of the Town isn't singled out for the quality of its cheesesteaks—but because the waitress calls the author honey and sweetheart. This makes Buschel feel all nostalgic about Philly until a truck driver who hasn't showered and shaved in days comes in and gets a honey *and* a wink.

TO GET THERE: From I-76 E, take the Passyunk Avenue/Oregon Avenue exit. Follow the signs for Oregon. Drive on Oregon about 12 blocks, then take a right onto Broad. Talk of the Town will be one light up on the right. By public transportation, take the Broad Street subway to the Stadium stop and walk half a block north on Broad Street.

SEATING: 4 tables and 2 booths

OFF-STREET PARKING: Yes

ALCOHOL: No

HOURS: 10 a.m. to midnight Sunday through Thursday, until 2 a.m. Friday and Saturday

ROLL: Amoroso's loaf, cut to 9 inches

MEAT: Steer rib-eye, thick-sliced in-house

ONION: Spanish, cut to a quarter-inch dice and cooked in batches

CHEESE: American or provolone, melted on the meat; or real Cheez Whiz, placed on the bread (although De Salis says he does use a weaker, copycat cheese product on fries)

GRILL SEASONING: Oil blend

SPECIALTIES: Old-Fashioned pizza steak made with tomato slices instead of sauce

WHAT'S WIT THE WHIZ?

Next to ordering incorrectly, Cheez Whiz is the thing cheesesteak newbies fear most. "They don't know what it is. They're afraid of it," says Patrick Dougherty of Steaks on South.

They're not the only ones. A good number of steak shop operators also want no part of the Whiz. "We only serve real cheese," says Vonda Bucci of John's Roast Pork of her shop's provolone and American cheese, although American is also processed. In fact, both Chez Whiz and American are part of

a long, proud American tradition of scientific manipulation to make cheese last longer, smell sweeter, and melt more easily—in short, to develop the improvements on "real" cheese that are credited with the eightfold increase in Americans' cheese consumption since James Kraft invented processed cheese in 1916.

Kraft came up with a method of extending cheese's shelf life on his kitchen stove mainly as a way to increase his Chicago wholesale cheese business. But once the U.S. government got wind of his new product, they bought six million tons to feed the soldiers during World War I. After the war, Kraft did almost as well selling the sandwich-shaped five-pound loaves to grocery delis. But when the grocers did the slicing, the cheese lost its brand identity and also some of its freshness. Hence the 1947 birth of American cheese "singles," an 80 percent cheddar cheese product sliced and wrapped by machines in the factory. White American is now the most popular cheese used to make cheesesteaks, and it's easy to understand why: it comes in convenient slices and contains stabilizers, emulsifiers, and flavor enhancers that extend the shelf life, mellow out the flavor, and allow the cheese to melt easily atop hot meat without clumping.

But the apex of the processed cheese production that launched and still sustains the Kraft food company came four years later. "Project Cheez Whiz," as it was dubbed in the Kraft newsletter at the time, began in 1951 and lasted almost eighteen months. The Kraft laboratory was originally aiming at the then-hot rarebit market (that's rarebit, not rabbit), which explains some of the rarebit ingredients such as mustard and molasses some Cheez Whiz versions still contain. But anticipating that this cheese-soaked bread dish would soon be about as unpopular as rabbit, Kraft's sales division asked dairy research manager Edwin Traisman and his colleagues to develop an all-purpose cheese sauce instead. It debuted on July 1, 1953, and was adopted at Pat's King of Steaks soon afterward, mainly for the speed and efficiency with which it could infuse a sandwich with cheese. (See chapter 1 for more on Cheez Whiz's introduction.) And though not as cheesy as American slices, the giant yellow cans of food service Cheez Whiz used by most local stands contain more than 51 percent of a combination of cheddar and Colby. That is at least 30 percent more "real" cheese than current-day supermarket Cheez Whiz dip and spread probably contain, says Bill Wendorff of the Wisconsin Center for Dairy Research at the University of Wisconsin–Madison. This doesn't necessarily mean Cheez Whiz is worse for you than 80-percent-cheese American or all-natural provolone. In fact, Wendorff says the whey that Kraft uses to partly substitute for real cheese in their less-expensive Cheez Whiz formulations actually contains better-quality proteins than more natural products. And a 1989 study conducted by one of Wendorff's University of Wisconsin colleagues suggested that this whey resulted in Cheez Whiz containing 6.5 times as much cancer-fighting conjugated linoleic acid (CLA) as cheddar cheese. Of course, the researcher presented the Cheez Whiz and cheddar to these unexpectedly healthy laboratory mice atop hamburgers. If he had fed the mice cheesesteaks, they all probably would have died from heart disease.

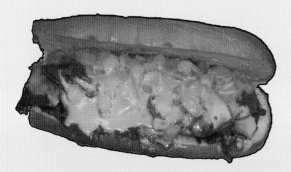

Cheez Whiz inventor Edwin Traisman. The reception following his 2007 memorial service featured Cheez Whiz canapés.

Tony Luke's
Old Philly Style Sandwiches

39 E. OREGON AVE., SOUTH PHILADELPHIA, 215-551-5725, WWW.TONYLUKES.COM

I n 1981 Tony Lucidonio Jr. was one of about 200 students at Philly's High School for the Creative and Performing Arts with aspirations to be the next Sylvester Stallone. Unlike the other 199, Tony also had the ingenuity to find out about the *Rocky II* wrap party being held in town and the chutzpah to crash it. There he was befriended by actor Burt Young, who told Tony to give him a call if he was ever in L.A.

Ever in L.A.? Within a few weeks, Tony had quit school and moved there. But the closest he ever got to fame was an angry phone call from actor James Caan (of *Godfather* renown), prompted by his going out with Caan's sister.

A discouraged Tony returned home and began working alongside his brother in his dad's food businesses, to live out the rest of his life in obscurity—or at least, this is the way most of these kinds of stories end. Instead, Lucidonio used his appearance in steak shop ads to launch a film and TV career as Tony Luke, resulting in so much Tony on stage and screen that he is, he says, "the Dave Thomas or Colonel Sanders of Tony Luke sandwiches," if not the national face of Philadelphia cheesesteaks generally. "In less than twenty years—in a very short period of time—we've become one of the top cheesesteak shops in town. And twenty years from now, when people think cheesesteaks anywhere in the world, they will also think Tony Luke's," the big, tattooed, bald-headed Luke vows.

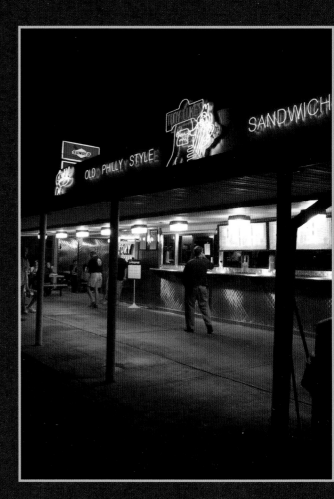

"I consider myself to be the Johnny Appleseed of cheesesteak. I intend to sprinkle fried onions across America."

Tony Luke Jr.

But that's getting ahead of the story. Tony worked in his dad's commissary business for about a decade before Tony Sr. decided to open a takeout stand featuring his family-famous roast pork sandwich. Broke after buying an old Oregon Avenue hot dog stand, Tony Sr. and his sons were forced to renovate the building themselves. The first year was touch-and-go, the next year only slightly better—until the Lukes acceded to customer demands for a cheesesteak and it won *Philadelphia* magazine's Best of Philly award in 1994, almost single-handedly doubling store sales.

Special events, including two "walk of fame" ceremonies honoring big-name entertainers with local roots and campy local cable TV ads that Luke Jr. wrote and starred in were also business boosters. One PG-rated ad shows Luke downing a huge meat-filled roll while a group of sexy women praise its size. His Forrest Gump parody caused a flurry of requests for Luke to pose with frat pledges. The ads also helped Tony land his first movie gigs, including his scene-stealing appearance as a crazed Eagles fan in *Invincible* (see side story).

But the audience for Luke's food was still largely local until Luke's Steak Italiano beat Bobby Flay's Strip Loin Poblano in a 2006 "Throwdown with Bobby Flay" episode on the Food Network. Now tourists come from all over to get that sandwich, Luke says just minutes before—as if on cue—a tourist spots Tony and asks him to pose for a picture. It's a newfound national visibility that Luke is trying to parlay into a nationwide chain of Tony Luke sandwich shops (he's already got three branches) and a line of frozen supermarket sandwiches.

Luke says, "There has long been this mentality that the only place you can get a good Philadelphia cheesesteak is in Philadelphia. I don't buy it. I consider myself to be the Johnny Appleseed of cheesesteak. I intend to sprinkle fried onions across America."

TONY LUKE JR. SELECTED FILMOGRAPHY

Tony Luke Jr. sums up his TV and film career thusly: "I usually play a bad guy who kills somebody and then they kill me. I die in almost all my movies."

Jamie Kennedy Experiment (2003). A Mob funeral setup.

Hack (2003). Luke plays a disgruntled vendor who kicks his machine in one episode of this Philly-lensed TV show.

10th and Wolf (2006). Luke is a Mob underboss who gets Dennis Hopper killed, only to get his comeuppance.

Invincible (2006). His first comic turn as an Eagles (right) fan trying out for the team got rave reviews. *Sports Illustrated* said: "[Luke] has more fun in that one scene than [Mark] Wahlberg appears to in his entire climb up the ladder."

The Happening (2008). Luke plays his food-stand-tending self in this M. Night Shyamalan thriller.

The Nail (2009). Luke stars in this fictional drama from his own story about an ex-boxer who accidentally kills someone in a bar fight. Directed by James Quattrochi and costarring William Forsythe.

TO GET THERE: From I-76 E, take the Passyunk Avenue/Oregon Avenue exit. Bear right onto Oregon. Go two and a half miles. Tony Luke's is located just past Swanson. By public transportation, take the Broad Street subway line to Oregon Station, then take Bus G (down Oregon to Front Street) or Bus 7 to Oregon and Vandalia.

OTHER LOCATIONS: Citizens Bank Park; 1 Citizens Bank Way, 215-463-1000; Borgata Hotel & Casino, 1 Borgata Way, Atlantic City, N.J., 609-317-1000; and 625 Rte. 33, Hamilton Township, NJ., 609-631-7400. (The Tony Jr.'s stand on 18th Street is unaffiliated, run by a former Luke's manager also named Tony.)

SEATING: At a few outdoor picnic tables (enclosed and with space heaters in the winter)

OFF-STREET PARKING: Yes, in an adjacent lot

ALCOHOL: Across the street at Tony Luke (Sr.'s) Beef and Beer Sports Bar

HOURS: 6 a.m. to midnight Monday through Thursday, 6 a.m. to 2 a.m. Friday and Saturday, 11 a.m. to 8 p.m. Sunday

ROLL: Parbaked custom Liscio's roll that is finished off on-site

MEAT: Steer rib-eye, thinly sliced, which breaks up when cooked

ONION: Chopped and precooked

CHEESE: Whiz or American (Tony Jr. is a Whiz proponent)

GRILL SEASONING: Canola oil, salt, and pepper

SPECIALTIES: Roast Pork Italian and Food Network–famed Steak Italian (both featuring spinach or broccoli rabe and sharp provolone cheese), the vegetarian Uncle Mike (sharp provolone, peppers, marinara sauce, fried onions, spinach, and broccoli rabe), and the Papa Luke (an offbeat Tony Jr. invention featuring steak, sliced tomato, and cream cheese)

STORY (AND I DO MEAN "STORY"): Even when he weighed 325 pounds, Tony Luke Jr.'s cholesterol has never gone above 165. His triglycerides are 45. His conclusion? "The secret to good cholesterol is cheesesteaks."

INDEX OF SHOPS BY FEATURES

ALCOHOL: Abner's, Campo's, Chubby's, Dalessandro's, Donkey's Place, Grey Lodge Pub, Jim's Steaks, Tony Luke's Beef & Beer Sports Bar

BIG EATERS: Abner's, Big John's, Gooey Looie's, John's Roast Pork, Larry's Steaks, Leo's Steaks, Lou's, Mama's Pizza, Pagano's Steaks & Hoagies, Pudge's

INDOOR SEATING: Abner's, Big John's, Campo's, Chick's Deli, Chink's, Chubby's, Claymont Steak Shop, Dakota Pizza Co., Dalessandro's, Donkey's Place, Grey Lodge Pub, Grilladelphia, Ishkabibble's, Jim's Steaks, John's Pizza, Larry's Steaks, Lou's, Mama's Pizza, Peppermill, Philip's, Pudge's, Shank's and Evelyn's, Sonny's Famous Steaks, Spataro's, Steaks on South, Steve's Prince of Steaks, Talk of the Town

OPEN LATE: Abner's, Chubby's, Claymont Steak Shop, Dalessandro's, Geno's, Grey Lodge Pub, Grilladelphia, Ishkabibble's, Jim's Steaks, Larry's Steaks, Leo's Steaks, Pagano's Steaks & Hoagies, Pat's King of Steaks, Philip's, Sonny's Famous Steaks, Steaks on South, Steve's Prince of Steaks, Talk of the Town, Tony Luke's Old Philly Style Sandwiches

SLAB-STYLE STEAKS: Campo's, Donkey's Place, Geno's, Grey Lodge Pub, Johnny's Hots, Pat's King of Steaks, Philip's, Rick's Steaks, Shank's and Evelyn's, Sonny's Famous Steaks, Spataro's, Steve's Prince of Steaks, Talk of the Town

WAITER/WAITRESS SERVICE: Big John's, Chink's, Chubby's, Dalessandro's, Donkey's Place, Grey Lodge Pub, Ishkabibble's, John's Pizza, Lou's, Mama's Pizza, Peppermill, Pudge's, Shank's and Evelyn's

CHAPTER 3

CHEESESTEAK ABROAD

PHILADELPHIANS VISITING TEXAS SHOULD BE CHOWING DOWN RIBS; WHEN IN MAINE, ENJOYING LOBSTER ROLLS; IN SEATTLE, SIPPING COFFEE. THEY SHOULD NOT WASTE THEIR TIME LOOKING FOR A GOOD CHEESESTEAK.

THAT SAID, THERE ARE TIMES WHEN PHILADELPHIANS MUST LEAVE THEIR NATIVE CITY FOR EXTENDED PERIODS—THESE DISPLACED SOULS JUSTIFIABLY SEEK A TASTE OF HOME. LIKEWISE, THERE ARE PEOPLE WHO DEVELOP A TASTE FOR REALLY GOOD CHEESESTEAKS WHILE VISITING PHILADELPHIA WHO WANT TO EXPERIENCE THAT TASTE AGAIN. THIS IS WHO THIS CHAPTER IS FOR. THE FOLLOWING PLACES COME RECOMMENDED BY PHILLY TRANSPLANTS AROUND THE COUNTRY AND THE WORLD. THE LIST IS ECLECTIC AND BY NO MEANS COMPLETE.

THIS CHAPTER IS ALSO THE PLACE TO FIND OUT ABOUT SOME CHEESESTEAK OFFERINGS FROM SUPERMARKET FOOD COMPANIES AND NATIONAL RESTAURANT CHAINS (AUTHENTICITY DEFINITELY NOT GUARANTEED).

LEGEND

AR = Amoroso's rolls
BB = birch beer
CS = cherry soda
GPC = Goldenberg Peanut Chews

HPC = Herr's Potato Chips
PMD = Philly memorabilia décor
TK = Tastykakes
WI = water ice

ARIZONA

CORLEONE'S

VARIOUS LOCATIONS, WWW.CORLEONES.NET

This Phoenix area chain serves up the stereotype of the South Philly Italian as mobster, along with self-described "killer" rib-eyes. "Truly a sandwich you can not refuse," its Web site says. **TK.**

DEFALCO'S ITALIAN DELI

2334 N. SCOTTSDALE RD., SUITE 133A, SCOTTSDALE, 480-990-8660, WWW.DEFALCOSDELI.COM.

The rib-eye sandwiches are made by the third generation of a Michigan Italian deli dynasty that nevertheless has lots of Philly expat fans.

PHILADELPHIA SANDWICH COMPANY

7158 E. FIFTH AVE., OLD TOWN, SCOTTSDALE, 480-970-1102, WWW.PHILLYCHEEZSTEAK.COM.

The Phoenix area's only twenty-four-hour steakery draws the post-bar crowd with promises to make you forget "you ever left Philly." Décor includes Philly murals and a framed snap of Cheez Whiz inventor Edwin Traisman. Mis-steak: "Second Street" specialty sandwich featuring french fries with mayo and provolone on a hoagie roll (I say this not because of the french fries but because, as far as I know, there are no vegetarians on Second Street). **PMD, TK.**

CALIFORNIA

LOS ANGELES

BIG MIKE'S PHILLY STEAK & SUBS

1314 HERMOSA AVE., HERMOSA BEACH, 310-798-1499; AND 507 MAIN ST., EL SEGUNDO, 310-726-9638

It's the old story: "Big" Mike Niemark couldn't find a good cheese-steak after moving from Jersey to Philly and so decided to do it himself. Unlike many other cheesesteak newbies, Niemark got tutoring from an expert (a slinger from Phil and Jim's in Parkside, Pennsylvania). He uses rib-eye and Italian rolls from a local bakery. Is it a mis-steak for Mike to say that locals tell him that his cheese-steaks are better than anything they've had in Philly (or is this just part of Mike's bigness)?

FREDOS PHILLYS

720 N. LAKE AVE., PASADENA, 626-798-9905, WWW.FREDOSPHILLYS.COM

This L.A. area favorite is owned by former East Coast biologist Daniel Cox and the shop's namesake and silent partner, Alfredo. Cox's bows to West Coast culture include barbecue- and teriyaki-flavored steaks. **AR, TK.**

PHILLY'S BEST

MANY LOCATIONS, WWW.EATPHILLYSBEST.COM

This Southern California chain of about two dozen shops is best known in Philly for a 2001 incident involving WPVI-TV (Channel 6) reporter David Henry. Out in L.A. for the 76ers-Lakers NBA finals, Henry had a hissy fit when Philly's Best owner Bob Levey agreed to an exclusive interview with an NBC-10 reporter instead of him. (Philadelphia area steak shop owners not named Vento or Olivieri wish they could get such attention.) Not connected to the Chicago chain of the same name. **AR, BB, CS, TK.**

PHILLY WEST BAR & GRILL

1870 WESTWOOD BLVD., 310-474-9787,
WWW.PHILLYWESTBARANDGRILL.COM

This divey Westwood bar offers beloved steaks, burgers, and an earful should anyone make the mistake of trying to order a Philly with Cheez Whiz from Laurie Lifland. "First of all, it's not called a Philly," Lifland says. "Secondly, it doesn't come with Whiz. We use real cheese here." Mis-steaks? Philly West also uses French bread because it's the best they can get. Also, the standard cheesesteak comes with marinara sauce as per custom in Allentown, where Laurie and her brother, owner Mark Lifland, are from. **PMD.**

SOUTH STREET

117 N. VICTORY BLVD., BURBANK, 818-563-2211, AND
1010 BROXTON AVE., WESTWOOD VILLAGE, 310-443-9895, WWW.SOUTHSTREETCHEESESTEAK.COM

Some ex-Philly-area movie types started this two-shop minichain that is heavy on Philly brand products and décor. They use Amoroso's rolls, rib-eye, and a somewhat unusual blend of melted American and provolone. South Street's Web site features the Orlons song of the same name on wearying continuous-loop play and, under the Accolades heading, information about a citation they received from the Philadelphia City Council (which is apparently what the council was doing when it should have been seeing to the pothole in front of your house). **AR, PC, PMD, TK.**

SAN DIEGO

ALEX'S BROWN BAG

2550 FIFTH AVE., 619-231-2912,
WWW.ALEXSBROWNBAG.COM

Alex is long gone. A guy named Benny from New York added cheesesteaks to the deli menu when he took over in the early 1980s, but according to current co-owner Jim Mullen, he didn't know what he was doing, "Well, he did a little bit," Mullen clarifies (apparently the steaks were good enough for Mullen to become a steady customer), "but he put way too much grease." Mullen fixed that when he bought Alex's with fellow Philly area expat Dave Sherako in 2000 and also injected a dose of Philly 'tude. Mullen proclaims, "We're loud for San Diego and we're also always right."

HERR'S PHILLY CHEESE STEAK FLAVORED KETTLE COOKED POTATO CHIPS

Most people eat Herr's potato chips with sandwiches. The cheesesteak is Philadelphia's most popular sandwich. But what if there were a cheesesteak-flavored potato chip? Eliminate the need for a cheesesteak and maybe people could just lunch on the chips!

Maybe—and then again, maybe not. After a gang-buster launch in March 2006, sales of Herr's Philly Cheese Steak Flavored chips dropped off and the product was discontinued—at least in the United States. The cheesesteak chips are still being sold some places overseas. (Which doesn't seem right somehow. It's one thing if nobody can get them. It's another if Tunisians can and Philadelphians can't.)

CALVIN'S WORLD FAMOUS SOUTH PHILLY CHEESESTEAKS & HOAGIES

1411 THE ALAMEDA, 408-286-5626

If not world famous, Calvin's was at least San Diego famous for its cheesesteaks from 1981 until the early 1990s, when Jonne Aleeson's last area steakery (named for his son) closed. In 2007 Alleson reopened just a few doors down from his original location, and at least some local cheesesteak lovers are rejoicing. They praise the authenticity of this South Philly native's food and gritty setting; detractors complain about the unappealing décor and slow service.

GAGLIONE BROS. FAMOUS STEAKS AND SUBS

724 VENTURA PLACE, 858-488-1690 AND 3944 W. POINT
LOMA BLVD., 619-758-0646, SAN DIEGO,
WWW.GAGLIONEBROS.COM

"We're not from Philly, we don't make a Philly cheesesteak, but we do make one that people have said is the best they've ever had," Joe Gaglione, one of three Gaglione brothers originally from the San Francisco Bay area, says boldly. They use chopped, sliced sirloin and Amoroso's rolls.

SAN FRANCISCO

CHEESE STEAK SHOP

MANY LOCATIONS, WWW.CHEESESTEAKSHOP.COM
Former Coatesville resident Keith Layton started this Northern California chain in 1982, but the California influence comes through in the shops' chili pepper and garlic cheesesteaks. Mis-steak: Full disclosure of nutritionals on its Web site. **AR, PMD, TK.**

JAKE'S

3301 BUCHANAN ST., SAN FRANCISCO,
415-922-2211, WWW.JAKESSTEAKS.NET
Philly native/ex-rower/options trader Jake Gillis opened this bar/steakery/hang out for homesick Philadelphians in 2005 but sold it a year later to—you guessed it—move back to Philly. **AR, PMD.**

JAY'S CHEESESTEAK

553 DIVISADERO ST., 415-771-5104; AND 3285 21ST ST.,
415-285-5200

Jay's is probably as well known for its seitan cheesesteak as the ones made from Niman Ranch beef. But in this epicenter of healthy eating, this might be more a survival strategy than a mis-steak.

SAN JOSE

AMATO'S

1162 SARATOGA BLVD., 408-246-4007,
WWW.AMATOSCHEESESTEAKS.COM
The son-in-law of the folks who ran Amato's Italian deli in Pennsauken, Bill Dill nevertheless takes pride in *not* flying in meat and rolls from Philly. As Bill told one poster on bestcheesesteaks.com, "Son, meat is meat. The cows here aren't any different than the cows on the East Coast. You just have to know what part to use." He uses top round and also picks up fresh rolls from a local bakery every morning to get around the local bakery custom of next-day delivery (in case you're wondering why the bread isn't as good elsewhere). **PMD.**

COLORADO

BOULDER

LARGE MARGE'S PHILLY CHEESESTEAK

3890 KIPLING ST., WHEAT RIDGE, 303-463-4549,
WWW.LARGEMARGES.NET
This popular little "joint" is run by South Philly native and ex-Mummer Marge Brown, who, at 125 pounds, is actually not all that large. Her homemade hot sauce dubbed Flaming Poo (inspired by a favorite defensive weapon in the movie *Madagascar*) is cooked on the grill with the meat in her signature Flaming Poo Steak. **AR, BB, CS, PMD, TK.**

DENVER

DENVER TED'S

1308 PEARL ST., 303-830-9089
Lancaster County native Ted Debruin owns this hipster cheesesteakery that is famed for its chocolate-covered Rice Krispies Treats and tables featuring built-in retro board games like Sorry. Mis-steak: "Traditional" steak sandwiches come with lettuce and tomato.

PAT'S PHILLY CHEESESTEAKS

THREE LOCATIONS, WWW.PATSCHEESESTEAKS.COM

This father-and-son-run minichain is most notable for its name. (Frank Olivieri Jr. of Pat's in Philly has talked about suing Pat Neelie.) Second mis-steak: Its "phine phriendly service" includes an apparent willingness to put oil, vinegar, mayonnaise, mustard, and/or ketchup on a cheesesteak.

PHILADELPHIA FILLY

FOOD WAGON, 16TH STREET MALL AT BROADWAY,

303-722-8722

The "filly" is Sally Rock, who went to the Restaurant School in Philadelphia before opening Denver's first cheesesteak restaurant in 1982. But she prefers the cart's shorter hours and simpler menu, which does not include Whiz. "We will not Whiz on anyone's sandwich," is how she puts it.

CONNECTICUT

DOOGIE'S

THREE LOCATIONS, WWW.DOOGIESHOTDOGS.COM

"Best Philly outside Philly" boasts Doogie's Web site, a statement backed up by the 800 to 1,000 cheesesteaks they sell each week. Doogie's owner Rock Aronheim claims no Philly connection—only that he uses the best Angus beef and freshest hard rolls he can find in Southern New England (although Aronheim's other culinary specialty is a sixteen-inch "monster" hot dog that makes anything he says hard to take seriously).

SUPER DUPER WEENIE

BLACK ROCK TURNPIKE, FAIRFIELD, 203-334-DOGS,
WWW.SUPERDUPERWEENIE.COM

Another Connecticut hot dog stand with a sidelight cheesesteak. Classically trained chef Gary Zemola makes his Pharifield cheesesteak with sirloin and a grilled Portuguese roll. Mis-steak: Mayo is standard.

CARL'S JR. PHILLY CHEESESTEAK BURGER AND HARDEE'S PHILLY CHEESESTEAK THICKBURGER

Buoyed by the success of a burger topped with New York pastrami in 2004, Carl's Jr. looked south to Philly for their second meat-as-condiment offering. Philly Cheesesteak Burgers featured two ounces of thinly sliced steak atop a quarter to a half pound of burger meat, along with peppers, onions, and Swiss and American cheeses. Brother chain Hardee's Philly Cheesesteak Thickburger copycat product clocked in at 930 calories and 63 grams of fat and was introduced with an ad featuring cab drivers speaking with such thick Philly accents that subtitles were provided.

DISTRICT OF COLUMBIA

PHILADELPHIA CHEESESTEAK FACTORY

THREE LOCATIONS, WWW.PHILLYSTEAKFACTORY.COM

This little DC chain was started by brothers Peter and Basil Mossaidis, formerly of Overbrook, in 1993. Mis-steaks: The "Original Cheesesteak (Steak)" features mushrooms, sweet peppers, and onions—instead of just onions—and one too many "steaks" in its name. **AR, PMD.**

FLORIDA

BECKY'S PHILLY-ING STATION

5 INTERBAY AVE., PENSACOLA, 850-457-8542,
WWW.BECKYSPHILLYINGSTATION.COM

This one gets the prize for cutest name. Sides include fried green tomatoes, in case you've forgotten that you're not *really* in Philly.

COLONIAL CORNER

7201 N. 49TH ST., PINELLAS PARK
(CLEARWATER AREA), 727-541-4300

This little corner hoagie/steak shop makes some of the best cheesesteaks outside Greater Philly, according to *Philadelphia* magazine. Owner Joann Casciato offers several possible reasons: she's the granddaughter of the originator of the LaSpada Italian deli chain in Chester, they slice their own rib-eye and use fresh local rolls, and Colonial Corner is located only about four miles from the Phillies' winter training camp (so if it wasn't good they wouldn't have lasted five minutes).

Colonial Corner customers chow down in the shadow of Philly sports memorabilia.

DELCO'S ORIGINAL

1737 MAIN ST., DUNEDIN (TAMPA/ST. PETERSBURG AREA), 727-738-4700

Owner Ed Crowley used to run a LaSpada's in the Chester/Media area. **AR, HPC, TK.**

FAMOUS PHILLY'S BEEF AND BEER FAMILY SPORTS PUB

215 ST. JOE PLAZA DR., PALM COAST, 386-246-5010,
AND 5901 S. RIDGEWOOD AVE., PORT ORANGE,
386-767-6338, WWW.FAMOUSPHILLYS.COM

This "home of the Belly Bustin' Philly Cheesesteak" is owned by reformed Pennsylvanian Joe Trapuzzano and is reportedly packed for Eagles games. Mis-steak: Dessert menu features Philadelphia brand cheesecake, which, as we all know, was actually born in New York state.

LASPADA'S PHILLY CHEESESTEAKS & HOAGIES

2200 N. VOLUSIA AVE, ORANGE CITY, 386-774-6400,
WWW.LASPADAS.COM

The third generation of the family that ran hoagie and cheesesteak shops in Atlantic City and Parkside since the 1930s has been spreading the Whiz in South Florida since the 1970s. Yes, Florida is crawling with LaSpada's but these two (and one in Charlotte, North Carolina) are still run by people of that name. Mis-steak: Mary LaSpada blames Subway for forcing them to list cheesesteaks under the menu heading Hot Subs. **AR, BB, PMD, TK.**

SONNY'S FAMOUS STEAK HOAGIES

1857 N. 66TH AVE., HOLLYWOOD, 954-989-0561

Samuel "Sonny" Nigro was a partner in Philly's famous Superior Italian bakery until his late 1940s move to Florida and 1958 opening of this family-style restaurant, famous for cheesesteaks. They're made with fresh-sliced rib-eye, homemade marinara sauce, and most important, their own bread. Mis-steak: Calling the regular steak (without lettuce and tomato) a "steak hoagie." Sonny's son, current owner John Nigro, knows better but says that's how they're referred to down there.

WESTSHORE PIZZA & CHEESESTEAKS

42 LOCATIONS, WWW.WESTSHOREPIZZA.COM

"You no longer have to dream about it" is the enigmatic slogan of this mega chain reportedly founded in 1994 to bring "the taste of Philly" to Florida.

GEORGIA

WOODY'S FAMOUS PHILADELPHIA

981 MONROE DR., ATLANTA, 404-876-1939

Pittsburgh native David Pastoria credits summers in Wildwood for the inspiration to add cheesesteaks to the menu of his ice cream shack (named after his late dog) in 1975. Thirty years later, people who by all rights should be eating grits stand in line to get one "all the way," which means dressed in mustard and ketchup, as per local preference. Killer banana milk shakes and orange freezes are vestiges of Woody's ice cream stand origins.

HAWAII

ONO CHEESE STEAK

2310 KUHIO AVE., HONOLULU,
808-923-8080,
WWW.ONOCHEESESTEAK.COM

The twenty-four-hour flagship stand and its twenty gas station and military base satellite locations are modeled on the Cheese Steak Shop chain in the Bay Area that Philippine native Joey Castaneda and his wife frequented before their move to paradise. Castaneda says he fends off challenges to their Philly cred with one word: "Amoroso." **AR.**

ILLINOIS

CHICAGO

PHILLY'S BEST

FOUR LOCATIONS, WWW.PHILLYSBEST.COM

"The only Philly cheesesteak in Chicago," boasts the Philly's Best Web site. And in his August 2005 survey of cheesesteaks elsewhere, Andrew Putz of *Philadelphia* magazine gave Upper Darby transplant Michael Markellos's cheesesteaks a thumbs up, though I'm not sure what a true Philly denizen would make of his oven-baked South Street Beef Grinder (inspired, Markellos says, by youthful visits to Upper Darby's New England Pizza) or the garlic bread cheesesteak roll alternative (because Markellos likes garlic).

MCDONALD'S PHILLY CHEESESTEAK SANDWICH

Philly area McDonald's franchise owner Chuck McIntyre spent three years studying cheesesteaks from local stands, including his favorite, Dalessandro's, before his Philly Cheesesteak Sandwich was offered at all six hundred Philadelphia area McDonald's in late 2003. Nevertheless, *Philadelphia Inquirer* restaurant critic Craig LaBan blasted its "squishy, overly sweet" too-small bun and "greasy" meat "studded with unchewable gristle." McIntyre's reaction? He said that purists "are going to have a problem with any cheesesteak that isn't made by a guy in a dirty T shirt sweating into the meat." At the same time, he admitted to some technical problems involving the way the steak meat was packaged: "It came in a bag that produced five sandwiches and if, after a half hour, the store hadn't sold that many, they would have to either throw it out or keep using it to make very bad sandwiches." Still, McIntyre thinks corporate should have given his creation longer than nine months.

KANSAS

CHARTROOSE CABOOSE

THREE LOCATIONS, WWW.CHARTROOSECABOOSE.NET

These locally popular branches of a national chain with a train theme specialize in cheesesteaks and frozen custard. Mis-steak: Swiss is the default cheese.

MARYLAND

CAPTAIN HARVEY'S SUBMARINES

1543 MERRITT BLVD., DUNDALK (GREATER BALTIMORE), 410-288-8990, WWW.STEAKSUBS.NET

For more than fifty years, Captain Harvey's has served up one of the Baltimore area's most popular and, perhaps not coincidentally, largest steak subs (as they are locally known). Takeout only.

JENO'S

552 BALTIMORE BLVD., SEVERNA PARK,
410-544-1416, WWW.JENOSSTEAKS.COM

"Anne Arundel county's finest cheesesteak" is the modest claim of this Filipino-American-owned-and-run steakery, and I'm betting a finer Asian Persuasion Cheesesteak (featuring cabbage, onions, mushrooms, and Asian sauce in addition to the usual meat and cheese) can not be found anywhere. Note to Joey Vento's counsel: The place is named for the daughter of founder Rodolfo Adriano and pronounced with a soft *e*.

MAGERKS PUB & GRILL

1061 S CHARLES ST, BALTIMORE, 410-576-9230
AND 120 S BOND ST, BEL AIR, 410-638-7701,
WWW.MAGERKS.COM

MaGerks was started by two brothers from Philly who were looking for a friendly place in Maryland to watch Eagles games. They ended up with two places that specialize in cheesesteaks. The shops also offer cheesesteak egg rolls and a MaGerk, which is a sandwich that sounds suspiciously like a McNally's Schmitter® (see page 167). **AR.**

SOUTH STREET STEAKS

7313 BALTIMORE AVENUE, COLLEGE PARK, 301-209-7007,
AND 12207 DARNESTOWN RD, GAITHERSBURG,
WWW.SOUTHSTREETSTEAKS.COM

Villanova native Jamie Rash opened his first South Street Steak in College Park in 2004 to sell cheesesteaks and to educate the locals about authentic ones. Now he's just selling cheesesteaks or actually, technically, cheesesteak hoagies with mayonnaise, as per local preference. People who eat two in one sitting get listed on the shop's Wall of Fame. **AR, PMD, WI.**

MASSACHUSETTS

BOSTON

CARL'S SUBS & BURRITOS

55 PROSPECT ST., WALTHAM, 781-893-9313,
WWW.THECHEESESTEAKGUYS.COM

This shop (no relation to Carl's Steaks in New York) is the clear favorite for what are locally known as steak bombs. I can't explain how the place can also make equally good Mexican food (espe-cially since the Lando family is Italian), but this influence can be seen in their Mexican cheesesteak (featuring cherry peppers, jalapeños, and Tabasco).

PINOCCHIO'S PIZZA AND SUBS

74 WINTHROP ST., HARVARD SQUARE (CAMBRIDGE),
617-876-4897, WWW.PINOCCHIOSPIZZA.NET

The so-called steak and cheese is a favorite at this small and crowded spot patronized by Harvard kids who call this The Noch. And aren't they supposed to be really smart?

T. C. LANDO'S SUBS & PIZZERIA

THREE LOCATIONS, WWW.THECHEESESTEAKGUYS.COM

This place is owned by the same family as Carl's of Waltham, but here the steaks are paired more conventionally with pizza.

MICHIGAN

JOEY'S FAMOUS PHILLY

14625 NORTHLINE RD., SOUTHGATE, 734-281-4444, AND
16125 WEST RD., WOODHAVEN, 734-692-1111,
WWW.JOEYSFAMOUSPHILLY.COM

"We're not asking you to be a Philly fan, just eat like one" is the defensive slogan South Philly native Sherri Abbulone came up with after convincing her husband, Joey, to convert his Red Wings–territory pizza shop into an emporium of Eagles fan favorites, including rib-eye steaks on Amoroso's rolls, hoagies, and crab fries. The educational component of their operation includes the menu notation that "any steak can be ruined wit Italian dressing" for an extra fifty cents., **AR, BB, CS, GPC, HPC, PMD, TK.**

Joey and Sherri with their twins in the shop.

MISSOURI

GRINDERS

417 E. 18TH ST., KANSAS CITY, 816-472-5454,
WWW.CROSSROADSKC.COM

This bar/diner/bohemian hangout is located in the heart of Kansas City's Crossroads Art District and owned by sculptor, Philly native, and major character Jeff "Stretch" Rumaner. Online posters give its cheesesteaks, which come with optional Whiz and Tater Tots, mixed reviews, especially compared to its signature thin-crust pizza. "Better than nothing," which is what most other area eateries offer, seems to be the main sentiment. Mis-steaks: According to rumor and one waitress, the "steak" meat is roast beef. **AR.**

NEBRASKA

DAVINCI'S

SIX LOCATIONS, LINCOLN. WWW.DAVINCIS.COM

The Web site features audio Italian lessons. Methinks they should study Italian-American Philly cuisine and get that Swiss off the cheesesteaks.

NEVADA

CAPRIOTTI'S

MANY LOCATIONS, WWW.CAPRIOTTIS.COM

This national chain has its roots in The Union Street, Wilmington, Delaware, sandwich shop. Its Web site lists cheesesteaks alongside hamburgers under Hot Subs. Capriotti's logo features a turkey, which might give you an idea of the best sandwich to order there.

POP'S

501 S. DECATUR BLVD., LAS VEGAS, 702-878-6444,
WWW.POPSCHEESESTEAKS.COM

"I've never been to Philly and never wanted to be in the restaurant business," Perry Walton declared in mid-2008. He ended up with this 1960s-era A-frame Weiner Schnitzel building as part of a failed business deal. Nevertheless, Walton takes pride in his 24/7 "Pride of Philly Steak" stand, which is appreciated by many Philly expats, including bestcheesesteaks.com Web site founder John Russ (who wrote his paean to Pop's before Walton bought that site). Walter's devotion is

---

> ### DOMINO'S PHILLY CHEESE STEAK PIZZA
>
> Domino's launched this steak-onions-peppers-mushrooms-and-provolone pizza nationally in fall 2003 with the endorsement of Pat's owner Frank Olivieri Jr. Sales were so good that the company violated, for the first time ever, its rule of never extending limited-time-products. The pizza has returned to national menus several times since, including in a 2007 mock battle with Domino's Brooklyn Style Pizza (for the title of Most-Watered-Down Ethnic Food?).

evident in his Pop's Web site's exegesis on "how to make a perfect cheesesteak," complete with ruminations on the virtues of marination and the difference between steak chopping and pulling. **AR.**

NEW JERSEY

(SEE ALSO CHAPTER 2 ON PAGES 36, 40 AND 58 AND "SHORE TOUR" ON PAGE 142.)

WILLY'S

21 MOMMOUTH ST., RED BANK, 732-933-1957,
WWW.WILLYSSTEAKS.COM

Willy's is a Jersey reincarnation of a family rib-eye steak business that started in Pittsburgh in 1957.

NEW YORK

NEW YORK CITY

99 MILES TO PHILLY

94 THIRD AVE., 212-253-2700

Onetime Carl's manager tries and fails to beat the master, according to *Philadelphia* magazine, which said, "If 99 Miles to Philly was a city, it would be Des Moines" (although one Web poster praised their waffle fries).

BB SANDWICH SHOP

120 W. THIRD ST., 212-473-7500

High-end chef Gary Thompson reinvented himself after 9/11 with this Greenwich Village lunch spot serving a tweaked version of the Donkey bar's oniony rib-eye on a poppy seed kaiser (see page 58) to widespread acclaim and outrage (from those who know where he got the idea and those who never heard of a cheesesteak on kaiser).

CARL'S

507 THIRD AVE., 212-696-5336 AND 79 CHAMBERS ST., 212-566-2828,, WWW.CARLSTEAKS.COM

Ex-dot-commer Carl Provenzano's frequent trips to visit the in-laws in Philly paid off not just in marital bliss but also in what is widely considered the best traditional cheesesteak served in the Big Apple.

PHILLY SLIMS

789 NINTH AVE., 212-333-3042

The name alone would be enough to scare most cheesesteak fans away. And yet Philly Slims supposedly offers an indulgent triple cheese (with Whiz, American, and provolone). BB, TK.

WOGIE'S BAR & GRILL

39 GREENWICH AVE., 212-229-2171, WWW.WOGIES.COM

Aaron Hoffman pays tribute to his late dad, Wogie, and Wogie's native Philly with cheesesteaks and draft Yuengling.

SCHENECTADY

MORRETTE'S KING STEAK HOUSE

1126 ERIE BLVD., 518-370-0555, WWW.MORRETTES.COM

Tony Morrette stopped at a Philly steakery while driving through Philly one day in the late 1940s and was inspired to start a business.

NORTH CAROLINA

ARTHUR'S

4400 SHARON ROAD, CHARLOTTE, 704-366-6456, WWW.ARTHURS-WINE.COM

Arthur's could be the world's only cheesesteakery-cum-wine shop. The Arthur of the original downtown cheese shop is long gone, but the guys who bought him out are reportedly from Philly. And yes, you can get your steak with your choice from a wide selection of wines by the glass. Mis-steak: All steaks come with lettuce and tomato.

GHASSAN'S FAMOUS STEAK SUBS AND KABOBS

THREE LOCATIONS, GREENSBORO, WWW.GHASSANS.COM

Ghassan's has accomplished in Greensboro what would be impossible in Philadelphia: it has become famous for its cheesesteaks and been named Best Heart Healthy restaurant. "We know a lot of customers following a weight management program who attested to successfully attaining their goal by sticking to a daily meal from Ghassan's," its Web site boasts on the page about this award. I'm betting those customers are eating the kababs.

IP3 (ITALIAN PIZZERIA III)

508 W. FRANKLIN ST., CHAPEL HILL, 919-968-4671, WWW.ITALIANPIZZERIA3.COM

As if pushing nonchain pizza in the South wasn't challenge enough, the Marrone brothers of Naples decided to also sell cheesesteaks they tried in Trenton and Philly when they lived in Brooklyn. Now brother Anthony says they sell 140 pounds of steak a week.

OHIO (SEE "BUCKEYE RIB-EYE") ⬛▶

BUCKEYE RIB-EYE

The best cheesesteaks in America are made in Philadelphia. And yet the most successful national Philly cheesesteak chains were born in Ohio. Why? Some say one big reason cheesesteaks are so good in Philadelphia is because they're the product of mom-and-pop shops, with family members on hand to monitor quality. But the skills needed to make a great cheesesteak or run a single stand are not what are needed to run a great franchise operation. For that, franchise experts say, you need a proven formula and a great training program, as well as marketing and other types of ongoing support that will keep franchisees in the fold long after they've learned how to make a cheesesteak.

Pat Olivieri's son found that out the hard way. With the "help" of former Sears and Burger King executives, Herb Olivieri tried and failed to successfully franchise the most famous name in cheesesteaks twice in the 1980s (see page 103). Philly Mignon was another local 1980s cheesesteak chain effort that derailed.

One problem with locally based franchise efforts is that they tend to want to begin their chains locally, where there is keen competition from well-established neighborhood shops. This was not a problem Wilmington, Delaware, native Ken Smith faced when, inspired by his youthful cheesesteak-eating experiences, he decided to open a cheesesteak shop in Columbus, Ohio, in 1982. His Steak Escape stand, now a chain, was pretty much the only cheesesteak restaurant in Ohio until the owner of a nearby restaurant, seeing its success, opened a similar place in Dayton the next year, which eventually grew into the Great Steak & Potato Company chain. Penn Station followed in Cincinnati in 1985, and Charley's Grilled Subs in Columbus in 1986. All four follow Steak Escape's original menu of traditional cheesesteaks and not-so-traditional hand-cut fries and fresh-squeezed lemonade, and all are still in business—although the franchise landscape has changed quite a bit since the 1980s. One change is the increased competition from bigger national restaurant chains like Quiznos, Subway, and Chili's, which have recently added cheesesteaks to their menus. And with fewer malls being built, these chains have had to use freestanding buildings or military base, airport, and college campus locations to fuel their growth. And grow they do, for the most part pretty much everywhere except Greater Philly. As Philadelphia *Metro* columnist Arthur Etchells once suggested, the only acceptable chain to locals is the one "around Vito's neck as he chops your steak."

OREGON

PORTLAND

FORD'S ON FIFTH

121 NW FIFTH ST., 503-226-2828

The grandson of the owner of the locally famous old Henry Ford's restaurant carries on, making, among other things, a locally respected cheesesteak with top round, French bread, and provolone cheese.

GRANT'S PHILLY CHEESESTEAK

15350 NE SANDY BLVD., 503-252-8012

Grant's makes its own potato chips and steaks with a wide variety of cheese toppings (including cream cheese and Tillamook cheddar). AR, TK.

PHILADELPHIA'S CHEESESTEAKS AND BREWPUB

6410 SE MILWAUKIE AVE., (503) 239-8544, AND 18625 HWY 43, (503) 699-4130, WWW.PHILLYPDX.COM

Philly area native Steve Moore and his wife, Amelia, were pioneers with cheesesteaks in this part of America in 1987. Since 1994, when Philadelphia's became Oregon's smallest licensed microbrewery, locals have been able to wash them down with beers like 2 Street Stout and Betsy Ross Golden.

PENNSYLVANIA
(EXCLUDING PHILADELPHIA AREA)

CAPTAIN GUS'S STEAK SHOP

600 W. ORANGE ST., LANCASTER, 717-392-9929

The so-called Pat's of Lancaster. Marinara sauce is standard.

BRASS RAIL RESTAURANT

3015 LEHIGH ST., ALLENTOWN, 610-797-1927, WWW.BRASSRAILRESTAURANT.COM

Phil Sorrentino opened the Brass Rail Restaurant in 1931, but as its Web site says, "The biggest year in Brass Rail history was 1937; that was the year Phil introduced Allentown to its first steak sandwich." That sandwich comes standard with fried onions, marinara sauce, pickles, and hot peppers, and is still this sit-down family

TRADER JOE'S PHILLY CHEESESTEAK PIZZA

Trader Joe's didn't want to talk about this product, which it introduced in 2007. No wonder, considering that it's made with roast beef, yellow peppers, and pepper Jack cheese (among its four cheeses).

restaurant's best seller, according to Phil's grandson and current owner Mark Sorrentino.

PRIMANTI BROS.

MANY LOCATIONS, PITTSBURGH, WWW.PRIMANTIBROS.COM

In history, hours, and belovedness, Primanti's original Strip District restaurant is Pittsburgh's Pat's. And Primanti's Pitts-burgher Cheesesteak is its best seller. But this is not a cheesesteak as anyone else defines it but rather ground sirloin steak (that is, hamburger) topped with cheese and Primanti's s Primanti's signature french fries, coleslaw, and tomato topping. Don't say I didn't warn you.

RHODE ISLAND

CHELO'S HOMETOWN BAR & GRILL

TEN LOCATIONS, WWW.CHELOS.COM

This popular local chain of family restaurants has a cheesesteak on its menu, although Chelo's is probably even better known for its fish and chips, burgers, and Delmonico steak sandwich.

SOUTH CAROLINA

PHILLY'S

4650 LADSON RD., SUMMERVILLE (CHARLESTON AREA),
843-873-0776, WWW.PHILLYSCHEESESTEAKS.COM

"You could go to Philadelphia or you could go down the street," is the scatological slogan of this South Carolina steak shop started by the Castellucci family, formerly of South Philly. The menu looks pretty authentic, but the steak pictures are the best argument for professional food photography I've ever seen.

SOUTH DAKOTA

MUGGSY'S SUB GALLERY

821 BROADWAY ST., YANKTON, 605-665-2241

In 2004 *Maxim* magazine dubbed Muggsy's steak and cheese one of the Ten Best Sandwiches in America. *Maxim's* editors are idiots, *Philadelphia* magazine's Andrew Putz concluded after trying one. But I wouldn't be at all surprised if Muggsy's serves the best cheesesteak in Yankton.

TENNESSEE

HEAVENLY HOAGIE

1428 UNION AVE., MEMPHIS, 901-726-0303,
WWW.HEAVENLYHOAGIE.COM

The barbecue is wonderful but the sandwiches are pitiful, Pete Cammarano discovered after moving from Reading, Pennsylvania, to Tennessee five years ago. Heavenly Hoagie is his antidote, widely praised by Philly expats for its rib-eyes as well as its great beer selection (including Yuengling) and fresh-cooked potato chips. **PMD.**

LENNY'S

MANY LOCATIONS, WWW.LENNYS.COM

This national Jersey-style sub chain started in Tennessee in 1998 and has more than forty shops in the state (although the owners got their sandwich start running a sub stand on the Wildwood boardwalk).

THE PURPLE COW

1648 E. STONE DR., KINGSPORT, 423-245-1707

The popular drive-through is known for its long lines, milk shakes, hamburgers, and steak "bombs." Cheesesteak may not be traditional fare for Southerners, but "they sure do order it, honey," said a worker at the place, between alarms warning her the fresh bread was ready. Owner Mike Warren says the shop sells 500 to 600 a day. Why the Purple Cow? "My wife likes purple," Warren explains. "And most of the food we serve is from a cow."

TEXAS

BILLADELPHIA

4105 AIRPORT FREEWAY, BEDFORD, 817-684-8607, AND
1112 N. COLLINS ST., ARLINGTON, 817-275-2199,
WWW.BILLADELPHIA.COM

"We'll change your y'all to yo!" Bill Walter promises on his menu. At least this South Philly native is *trying* to give locals real steaks rather than Philly-style or Philly-like ones. But it's a battle. Walter laments, "They want to put everything on it you can imagine: mustard, mayo. I used to get angry." Now he mostly complies, though he draws the line at jalapeños. But Philly transplants call this old hot dog stand and newer sports bar a taste of home. **TK, HPC, BB, PMD.**

The Billadelphia takeout stand: too cute to serve cheesesteaks?

DELAWARE SUB SHOP

VARIOUS LOCATIONS, WWW.DELAWARESUB.COM

Wilmington native and ex-accountant Pete Ademski credits Delaware's Casapulla's sub shops for the concept and spokesman Jerry Sisemore for much of the success of his nineteen-year-old central Texas cheesesteak chain. As a former University of Texas all-American and a former Eagle, Sizemore has both Philly and Texas cred. The rib-eye steaks come standard with white American and ketchup as per Wilmington tradition. **AR, TK, PMD.**

FRED'S DOWNTOWN PHILLY

3017 N.BELTLINE RD, 214-492-1226, IRVING, AND 1144 N.PLANO RD, RICHARDSON, 972-437-0054, WWW.PHILLYCHEESESTEAKS.NET

"The best 10 inches you've ever had in your mouth," boasts ex-Philadelphian Fred Daniels of his cheesesteaks (I hope) at a Web address that half the steak slingers in Philly would probably give their eye roll for (so he is definitely smart in some ways). The Web site features a section of cheesecake snaps called Our Women Patrons and pictures of hunks of provolone and American cheese. If the in-person experience is only half as interesting . . . **PC, PMD, TK.**

VIRGINIA

AL'S STEAK HOUSE

1504 MT. VERNON AVE., ALEXANDRIA, 703-836-9443, WWW.ALSSTEAK.COM

The *Washington Post* has deemed Al's the "best Philly style cheesesteaks in the area" and Web posters, including bestcheesesteaks.com editor John Russ, who lived in the area for a while, agree. The place was started by the South Phillyite Al Martino (not the singer) in 1956; current owner John Severson took over in 1965 and is a bit curmudgeonly—in other words, well qualified. The small menu includes that rare sop to the health conscious, the turkey cheesesteak. Mis-steaks: All steaks come with shredded lettuce. Provolone is called "Roman cheese."

COPPOLA'S DELICATESSEN

2900 W. CARY ST., RICHMOND, 804-359-6969, WWW.COPPOLASDELI.COM

Tom Roukous's twenty-five-year-old recipe for cheesesteaks includes hot and sweet peppers, provolone, and mustard and ketchup (but he is originally from Rhode Island).

BETTY CROCKER HAMBURGER HELPER PHILLY CHEESESTEAK

Those without the time or skill to make the cheesesteak casserole in the DIY chapter might want to seek the help of Hamburger Helper's Philly Cheesesteak flavor, which debuted in 2000 and, according to a company spokesperson, sells better in the Philadelphia area than in the rest of the country (so maybe it's actually good). The R&D person behind it said he modeled the formulation after cheesesteaks he had seen "on the East Coast, with a preference toward a milder provolone cheese taste with onions and green peppers" and that the unorthodox french fried onion topping was for "textural contrast."

FOREST RESTAURANT

5057 FOREST HILL AVE., RICHMOND, 804-233-1940, WWW.DOITINTHEFOREST.COM

This bar boasts of its "famous" cheesesteak, a description confirmed by at least a few Web postings.

WASHINGTON

PHILLY BILMOS

2100 SE 164TH AVE., VANCOUVER, 360-944-1006, WWW.PHILLYBILMOS.COM

Parsippany, New Jersey, native Michael Bitter stocks his far-West flat-top grill with authentic Original Philadelphia Cheesesteak Company meat and Amoroso's rolls. The Bilmos name is made up and meaningless, to the disappointment of people who ask Bitter about it daily (but it *is* a better name for a foodery than Bitter). **AR, PMD, TK.**

PHILLY FEVRE STEAK & HOAGIE SHOP

2332 E. MADISON ST., SEATTLE, 206-323-1000,
WWW.PHILLYSTEAKSHOP.COM

This pioneering out-of-state steak shop started by Renee LeFevre (hence the name) is now owned by another former Philadelphian, Edwina Martin, who reportedly had her first date with her husband there. So the menu's pretty traditional—the sukiyaki cheesesteak (featuring steak, peppers and mushrooms, and soy sauce) excepted. **PMD, TK.**

TAT'S EAST COAST STEAKS & SUBS

115 OCCIDENTAL AVE., SEATTLE, 206-264-TATS,
WWW.TATSDELI.COM

Penn State buddies Brian Tatman and Jason Simodejka opened this little living museum of East Coast sandwiches on Seattle's Pioneer Square in 2004. They use top round for the cheesesteaks, but their best seller is actually a New York–Philly hybrid pastrami cheesesteak, Tat'strami, which consists of thin-sliced, chopped, and grilled pastrami served with coleslaw, Swiss cheese, and Russian dressing. **TK.**

Shop namesake Brian Tatman (right) and partner Jason Simodejka

WEST VIRGINIA

JERSEY'S

1756 MILEGROUND RD., MORGANTOWN, 304-292-2796

North Jersey native Matt Crimmel's shop-sliced bottom round has given area Mid-Atlantic transplants a reason to stay.

WISCONSIN

THE PHILLY WAY

405 S. SECOND ST., MILWAUKEE, 414-273-2355,
WWW.THEPHILLYWAY.COM

Ex-Philly radio man Dave London has been showing Wisconsinites the right way to eat cheesesteaks since 2002—that is, the Philly way, or as London puts it, "Don't ask me for red sauce and mayo and other crap." Despite this attitude or maybe because of it, he says sales of his rib-eyes have "gone like a rocket since day one." **TK, AR, HPC.**

LEAN POCKETS PHILLY STEAK & CHEESE

Philly Steak & Cheese is obviously a favorite flavor variety of food scientists at Nestle, the company behind five frozen cheesesteak-flavored products sold under the Hot Pockets or Stouffer's brand name. Hot Pockets introduced it first (in 2001), but the Stouffer's varieties are more popular. (The Philly-style Steak & Cheese is one of Stouffer's top-selling paninis.)

EXPRESS CHEESESTEAKS

One (expensive) alternative for people unhappy with the quality of cheesesteaks outside of Philly is direct mail. Here are some of the companies who do this and how it works.

CAMPO'S

WWW.CAMPOSDELI.COM, 215-923-1000

Mike and Denise Campo make the sandwiches like they do in their shop, freeze them, pack them in a cooler, and ship them with other Philly food favorites (Herr's chips, a Tastykake, a Philly soft pretzel) within twenty-four hours for between $70 (one cheesesteak) and $140 (for four).

PHILLY FOOD

WWW.PHILLYPRETZELS.COM, 610-566-4386

Joe Kubicky's Philly food care packages are a sideline of his catering company. He wraps his cheesesteaks in film and refrigerates them for a few hours before sending them off with ice packs. Expect to pay at least $100 for a cheesesteak, Tastykake, pretzels, and Goldenberg Peanut Chews and shipping.

STEAKS ON SOUTH

WWW.STEAKSONSOUTH.COM, 215-922-7880

Patrick Dougherty ships out cheesesteaks as a supplement to his South Street steak shop business. He packs the cooked meat separately from the rolls. Cost is about $10 per steak plus overnight shipping (which was $50 for one recent single-steak order delivered to Chicago).

JIM'S

WWW.JIMSSTEAKS.COM, 215-928-1911

Jim's is the only big-name Philly cheesesteak place that offers mail order. They deep-freeze the entire sandwich (without peppers or mushrooms, which don't freeze well) for three days and then ship it out for overnight delivery in a Styrofoam container. Three days' notice is required and the minimum order is eight steaks; expect to pay at least $100.

TASTE OF PHILADELPHIA

WWW.TASTEOFPHILADELPHIA.COM, 800-846-2443

Fred Catona is the originator of this little slice of the cheesesteak business (he's been doing it since 1978). The sliced roll and the cooked, made-to-order steak meat, cheese, and onions are sealed in separate plastic bags, packed in Mylar and placed in a Styrofoam cooler with ice packs. Customers of the basic $90 one-sandwich package also get Herr's chips, a Tastykake, two soft pretzels, and a "Yo, wha supp?" button (guts to wear it not included).

SO YOU WANT TO BE A STEAK SLINGER

Are you a Philly expat with no job or job prospects? Then do what so many former Philadelphia area residents are now doing: parlay your years of eating cheesesteaks in Philadelphia into a new career running an out-of-town cheesesteak shop.

In addition to knowing what a real cheesesteak is, requirements include an ability to ignore the 60 percent restaurant failure rate and the large number of broken links on the www.bestcheesesteaks.com Web site. Ballpark figures from cheesesteak shop chains suggest you will also need an initial investment of $200,000 to $300,000 (of your own money or borrowed or a combination).

You must also be willing to spend your workday talking about Philadelphia and Philadelphia sports teams—even if you moved away because you didn't like the place.

SHORE TOUR

Vacationing on the Jersey Shore doesn't have to mean cheesesteak withdrawal. Here are a few places, in order of how much they're praised, that can provide relief from all those frozen custards, pizzas, and hot dogs.

WHITE HOUSE SUB SHOP

2301 ARCTIC AVE., ATLANTIC CITY, 609-345-1564
This is probably the most famous place to get cheesesteaks—or steak subs, as they're called here—on the Shore, although they're not exactly like the ones in Philly. The superfresh bread, delivered on a near continuous basis from a bakery across the street, is French-like, hollowed out, and doused with a squirt of olive oil before being filled with the meat. People waiting in line for the nine booths and five stools entertain themselves by looking at the celebrity snaps and the towel Sinatra used during his last performance in Atlantic City (also framed and on the wall).

VOLTACO'S

957 WEST AVE., OCEAN CITY, 609-399-0743
The staff at this 1950s-era takeout Italian place can be curmudgeonly, but the cheesesteaks are highly praised.

RUSSO'S MARKET

NINTH AND SURF, NORTH WILDWOOD, 609-729-9318
The cheesteaks at this classic old Italian deli have many fans. Expect a wait.

SACK O' SUBS

VARIOUS SHORE LOCATIONS, WWW.SACKOSUBS.COM
White House relatlons own this minichain and the food is similar, say boosters like Frank Olivieri Jr. of Pat's.

DONKEY'S PLACE

1018 ASBURY AVE., OCEAN CITY, 609-399-9959
A franchised spin-off of the original Camden bar (see page 58).

STEAKS UNLIMITED

21 OCEAN TERR., SEASIDE HEIGHTS, 732-830-8830
This is a great place to get a steak, a beer, and a view of the boardwalk—and it's open into the wee hours.

CHAPTER 4:
CELEBRATING CHEESESTEAKS

THE MOST OBVIOUS WAY TO CELEBRATE CHEESESTEAKS IS TO EAT THEM. BUT WHAT IF YOU'RE FULL? THEN IT'S TIME TO ENJOY A CHEESESTEAK MOVIE OR SONG, SURF A CHEESESTEAK WEB SITE, PUT ON A CHEESESTEAK HAT, ATTEND A CHEESESTEAK EVENT, OR READ UP ON THESE THINGS IN THIS CHEESESTEAK BOOK.

THE DOCUMENTARY

Cheesesteaks have been the subject of many a TV news report but, so far, of only one documentary. Although Ben Daniels made *This Is My Cheesesteak* to fulfill requirements for his 2007 BFA in film from Syracuse University, the forty-minute film has already been featured at a number of film festivals, including the 17th Philadelphia Film Festival and the 2008 New York Food Film Festival, where it took home the Audience Choice award. And now it has the great honor of being included in this *Great Philly Cheesesteak Book*.

A food and a film lover, Daniels made a number of food-themed shorts in college, including one on the Pat's-Geno's rivalry. When he proposed a fictional feature about cheesesteaks for his senior thesis, his advisor countered, "You can't create characters that good." That's how he ended up making a documentary.

On multiple trips to Philly from school, Daniels interviewed the owners of Pat's, Jim's, Steve's, and Tony Luke's; took a motorcycle ride with Joey Vento of Geno's; and baked ziti and meatballs with the Bucci family of John's Roast Pork. But Daniels saves the greatest accomplishment of his film for the closing credits: getting all the above-named competitors to pose for a group photo. It was taken at an April 2007 "world premiere screening" of a rough cut of the movie at the Bridge Cinema in West Philadelphia by Daniels's dad, Ted, a photographer who has had his own movie career of sorts. (Ted can be seen eating a bagel in the background of a scene in the film classic *The French Connection*.)

Steak stand rivalry wasn't the only obstacle Daniels had to overcome to make *This Is My Cheesesteak*. There are also the facts that he grew up in a home with no TV and that he was a vegetarian from ages eight to nineteen, although he says he

Ben Daniels

made a ritual exception once every year "to have one real cheesesteak—after which I always got sick." Needless to say, he is now back to eating meat.

THE ANNUAL RANKING

Philadelphia magazine invented the annual Best Of awards that are now a standard feature for regional magazines around the country, and for most of the thirty-five years they've been granting them, Best Cheesesteak has been among the most closely followed categories. Tony Luke Jr. says winning it in 1994 almost single-handedly saved his stand after a struggling first year and a half; John Danze of Johnny Hots says the 2006 prize doubled his business. While it's possible to have a successful cheesesteak business without a Best of Philly nod, most of the stands generally considered the best have won it at least once.

How does *Philadelphia* wield its power on the local cheesesteak scene? In the Best Of's early days, shops delivered their sandwiches to the magazine's office for a taste-off. But current editor Larry Platt says that method has long since been abandoned in favor of staff picks informed by year-round reporting. At a certain point, writers and editors submit their lists of favorites in the various categories, the lists are compiled, and the internal lobbying begins. If there are any taste-offs, this is when they take place, in the form of staff members visiting the nominated steakeries anonymously, the way their readers would. At its best, this very subjective process unearths some hidden gems like 2003 winner Chick's Deli of Cherry Hill, New Jersey, and two-time winner Cosmi's Deli of South Philly, along with heated reader reaction—which is, Platt says, what you want. (He's in the business of selling magazines, after all.)

To further fuel the fire (or perhaps just defuse the furor over a single unpopular choice), the magazine has recently begun naming one city-based Best Cheesesteak winner and several subsidiary suburban ones. In 2004 and 2005 the cheesesteak prize also served as a launchpad for full-length feature stories about staff members' attempts to taste-test dozens of cheesesteaks around the region and the country. One odd result: steak shops in Wisconsin, Florida, and Chicago that can now boast of being Best of Philly.

Berman's cheesesteak hat

THE HATS

The rivalry between Pat's and Geno's is nothing compared to the one between the two major cheesesteak hat makers.

In one corner is Robert Berman, owner of Runnemede, New Jersey's $8 million Rasta Imposta novelty hat and costume company, which started making a fabric cheesesteak hat to cash in on the Eagles 2004 run at the Super Bowl.

In the other is Mike Paquin, a former bobblehead doll marketer from Lansdowne, Pennsylvania, who saw in the foam cheesesteak hat business a chance to marry his novelty products career and his love and personal obsession with cheesesteaks.

"His looks more like a chili-cheese-topped baked potato," says Berman of Paquin's hat.

"I'm not going to argue that ours looks *exactly* like a cheesesteak. But his is complete crap, garbage," Paquin counters. "Ours is far more durable and obnoxious, which is what products like this are for."

There is no argument about which came first: it's Paquin's, which he purchased from inventor Brett Koehler. Koehler modeled his cheesesteak hat on the Green Bay Packer cheesehead hats and was hoping to duplicate their success. Paquin first saw Koehler's hat at the Eagles' World's Largest Cheesesteak event (see page 149) in 1998 and approached Koehler shortly afterward, offering to become his sales manager. Koehler declined, but several years later, when he was ready to sell, Paquin was still interested.

Paquin had good timing, buying just before two exciting Eagles seasons. Sales were so good that he had to reorder— but then the factory that made the hats for him ran out of paint during production. Without notifying Paquin, the factory substituted another paint, which started flaking off. Paquin recalls, "I started getting returns. Things were smokin' hot and then everything fell apart."

At almost the same time, competitor Berman started overseas production of his cheesesteak hat, enabling him to undercut Paquin's retail hat price, which ranged from $35 to $40, by almost half.

"His Rasta hat is classic. I give him all the credit in the world for doing it," Paquin says of Berman's founding faux dreadlocks invention. "But his cheesesteak hat is really cheaply made," Nevertheless, many customers not as quality conscious as Paquin began buying Berman's $20 hat.

Paquin is not discouraged. On the contrary, he is planning a whole cheesesteak product line that would include cheesesteak antenna toppers, air fresheners, finger puppets, and windup toys to take advantage of his novelty-item-selling experience. Paquin also owns the rights to a hoagie hat he bought from someone else who "overestimated the market."

As for Berman, he says sales for his Rasta Imposta cheesesteak hat pale next to his banana costume: "Bananas are just funny. People buy it with a gorilla suit and then chase each other." He says that the cheesesteak hat, by contrast, "only sells when the Eagles are doing well." In other words, most of the time, fu-gettaboutit.

YOU CAN BUY BERMAN'S CHEESESTEAK HAT AT WWW.CHEESESTEAKHAT.COM; PAQUIN'S CAN BE FOUND AT WWW.PHILLYCHEESESTEAKHAT.COM.

THE FIRST WEB SITE

Cheesesteak deprivation is a powerful thing. In fact, it's powerful enough to make an infrequently updated, graphically static thirteen-year-old site one of the most popular cheesesteak destinations on the Web.

Bestcheesesteaks.com creator John Russ didn't even set out to create the definitive listing of best cheesesteak shops around the country. The site instead evolved organically from cyberdelphia.net, a Philadelphia sports destination that the native of Reading, Pennsylvania, who was then living in northern Virginia, created for fellow displaced fans. But so much discussion about where to find good cheesesteaks outside Philadelphia came up, that in 1996 Russ decided to do a cheesesteak site spin-off.

The site now features nearly three thousand picks and

pans, many of Zagat-like sharpness and candor. For instance, a posting for the Philadelphia Connection shop in Pasadena, California, says it's great "if you like tough steak, soggy rolls and limp onions . . . For me, it's PASS-adena." "THERE IS NO GOOD PHILLY STEAK SANDWICH IN THIS TOWN!" concurred another Los Angelino (emphasis his).

"I haven't had a Dalessandro's steak for twenty-five years, but I'll never forget how great they are," sighs Betty Weber Carroll of Maryland, while someone else rhapsodizes about Dalessandro's homemade roasted peppers' power to make "your eyes roll back into your head."

Most of the visitor comments and editor picks date back to the site's earliest days. In occasional subsequent postings, Russ apologized for not keeping things more up-to-date. In early 2007 Russ gave up the fight, selling the site to Las Vegas steak stand owner Perry Walton, who hopes to parlay its popularity into a platform for a new cheesesteak mail order business. Medical problems have prevented Walton from doing that or posting planned updates as fast as he would like. But he promises that changes will come and that they won't be mainly plugs for his Vegas shop and mail order business. Says Walton, "One of the things that makes this site so incredible is its objectivity. I won't be doing anything to damage that."

GOURMET CHEESESTEAK COMPETITION

It seems that you can't be considered a serious chef in Philadelphia unless you can come up with a high-end riff on the cheesesteak. This odd situation can be blamed on David Neff and the Gourmet Cheesesteak Competition he cooked up for the Wyndham Franklin Plaza hotel in 1996. In the mid-

Newspaper columnist and celebrity judge Stu Bykofsky looks before he eats.

1990s management at that hotel turned to the PR man for help in giving its restaurants a more upscale image. Neff came up with the idea of inviting journalists to the Wyndham to rate some of the city's best chefs' takes on the city's favorite sandwich. The popularity of the cheesesteak and the fact that the judges worked for local media outlets gave the contest almost instant renown.

In fact, the contest became such a local fixture that shortly after being named one of America's top ten new chefs by *Food & Wine* magazine in 1998, Guillermo Pernot of Pasion restaurant said that he was much better known locally as the Gourmet Cheesesteak Competition's defending champ. Neff says the "young, cocky, talented" chefs jumped at the chance to prove themselves in front of their peers and loved the challenge of turning the traditionally lowbrow food into haute cuisine. Indeed, the list of participants over the contest's six-year run is a who's who of Philly cuisine. In addition to Pernot, it includes Marc Vetri, Terence Feury, Chris Painter, Chris Scarduzio, and Walter Staib. Two-time winner Albert Paris, now of Mantra, told a newspaper reporter at the

John Anderson of Solaris Grille adds some mushrooms to the meat.

time, "It's a boxing match of chefs."

The hotel lobby cook-off format increased the drama and public interest. In keeping with the goal of upscaling the Wyndham's image, judges were given knives and forks and served by waiters in tuxes. Contest rules required each entry to feature the basic cheesesteak elements of beef, cheese, and bread, which made 1998 competitor Lance Holton of upscale fishery Striped Bass feel like, well, a fish out of water. "I haven't cooked a piece of meat in a year and a half so I have no idea what I'm doing," he admitted to Kathy Boccella of the *Philadelphia Inquirer* as he plopped five pounds of uncut beef tenderloin on a contest grill. Meanwhile, competitor Raul Bacordo of the Continental presented his Black Angus sirloin and mascarpone combination next to Chinese takeout boxes filled with crispy fries; Gerald Stenger of Caribou Café tried sirloin marinated in Burgundy and pesto topped with pepper goat cheese and snow pea shoots in tomato coulis; and Mike Stern created a sushi look-alike of traditional steak, cheese, and onion rolled up in a flatbread with hummus and pickled turnips. Other chefs used marinated yogurt cheese, Lebanese herb relish, cilantro, Jordanian chiles, and even Bugles corn chips.

Seven of this contest's concoctions were beautiful enough to be the subject of a two-page photo spread in the January 2000 *Philadelphia* magazine. As for their taste, well, let's just say none of these upscale chefs have opened steak shops, and no local steak shop has felt the need to add a Burgundy-pesto steak sandwich to its menu.

WORLD'S LARGEST CHEESESTEAK

In December 1998, with its team on the brink of setting a franchise record for losses in a single season, the management for the Philadelphia Eagles football team realized that an ordinary Fan Appreciation Day just wouldn't do. These fans deserved a very *big* thank you. And so before the very last game of that dismal season, Eagles promotions director Kim Babiak Phillips cooked up a scheme to create the world's largest helping of Philly fans' favorite food: cheesesteak.

After coming up with this idea, Phillips contacted Guinness to find out what would be involved. There was no category for cheesesteaks, but Phillips was told that to break the record for largest sandwich, the cheesesteak would need to be at least 301 feet long, feature at least three ingredients, and be made on one continuous piece of bread (no fair cobbling a bunch of rolls together with Cheez Whiz). The Eagles turned to Stroehmann Bakeries of Norristown for help with this last, most difficult requirement. After a number of parking lot practice bakes, Stroehmann production manager Tom Tuzzi settled on the idea of cooking the bread on-site in temporary ovens constructed of cinder blocks, covered with steel grating, and heated by propane. Tuzzi would mix the dough at the bakery, then pump it onto split PVC pipes that would be transported to the stadium in a refrigerated truck. Upon arrival, the pipes would be placed on the grates, and Tuzzi and four fellow bakers would knead the dough pieces together, section by section, before the propane tanks were revved up and aluminum foil covers put on for the big bake. Meanwhile, twelve local steak shops, including Talk of the Town, Slack's, Lee's, Tony Luke's, and Steve's, would each grill up a portion of the donated 475 pounds of steak meat to fill their thirty-foot section of the giant sandwich.

Tuzzi says that the test runs had left him pretty confident that "the bread would bake." What spoiled his holiday week, he says, was worrying about "what was going to happen when we tried to slice it." He remembers wondering, "Would it break and would we be disqualified with all the media and this guy dressed up like Grandpa Stroehmann there?"

Armed with a 19-point timed battle plan (9:00 a.m.: start cooking steak; noon: lay out dough; 1:20 p.m.: slice bread), Phillips also was not too worried—at least not until Christmas Day, when someone informed her that propane could freeze at 38 degrees. "Fortunately, it was in the forties that day," Phillips recalls a decade later with still-audible relief. The bread also did not break upon slicing, and at the 2:30 p.m. reckoning, the cheesesteak measured out at a world-record-breaking 360 feet (not coincidentally, the length of a football field). Then it was cut up and devoured by hungry fans, more than one of whom probably hoped coach Ray Rhodes might pick up some tips on executing a successful game plan from the cheesesteak-making team. (Yes, the Eagles lost the game that followed the sandwich snack 20-10.)

THE MOVIE SCENE

About halfway through the movie *Rocky*, two Philadelphia icons meet in a scene set at Pat's. In at least one version of the script, the scene opens with loan shark Gazzo and his halfhearted collector Rocky eating sandwiches. However, in the final cut, Gazzo only drinks a soda and Rocky just smokes a cigarette; then Gazzo, in a moment of softheartedness, donates $500 toward Rocky's fight training costs.

Rocky writer and star Stallone lived in Northeast Philadelphia for a time as a teenager, but Jodi Letizia, an actress from Philly who plays Marie in the movie, does not believe Stallone knew South Philadelphia very well and thinks her late father, Joe, who is credited as local "liaison" for the movie, suggested the Pat's location.

Harry and wife Anna Olivieri with Sylvester Stallone

THE SONG

Philadelphia's WIP sports radio station was behind one of the most significant recent cheesesteak stand surveys. That station is also responsible for the sandwich's song (thereby

adding further evidence to the widespread belief that cheesesteaks and sports go together like pepper pot soup and sherry).

"The Cheesesteak Song" was written by local musician and song-writer Skip Denenberg during his gig as "official songwriter" on WIP's morning show. Filling up four and a half hours a day with sports chatter isn't easy (especially when the Eagles are losing)—Denenberg's job was to create and perform songs about whatever the hosts are talking about, on the spot. That typically results in impromptu musical tributes to people like Vince Papale ("Lucky Man"), Tug McGraw ("Hero"), and Harry Kallas ("Out of Here"). But on one particular morning in 2005 when a show guest started talking about food, Denenberg started singing, "Sauté those onions. Grill up the meat. Cheez Whiz or provolone. Turn up the heat . . ."

The original version Denenberg sang that morning named six famous cheesesteak stands, including Tony Luke's. But the stand names are not in the Tony Luke Jr.–bankrolled, studio-produced CD version now being sold online and at souvenir shops (for $5). "We wanted to broaden its appeal as a tool for marketing the city to tourists," Denenberg explains.

That could also explain the somewhat questionable line "So when you come to Philly, we aim to please." (Well, OK, if you order your cheesesteak the *right* way, maybe). Ditto the way the refrain calls them *Philly* cheesesteaks (instead of just cheesesteaks), just like the tourists.

THE ARTICLE

By 2002, Craig LaBan had been restaurant critic for the *Philadelphia Inquirer* for four years but still had not written the big comprehensive story about the food his readers cared about the most. The "hot button" nature of the topic and doubts about his own physical ability to down so many kept him away until some students at Lower Merion High School asked for LaBan's help on a senior project to find the best local cheesesteak. LaBan accepted, thinking that the students' big appetites and company could make such an article both doable and fun.

Over four days in late spring 2002, LaBan and his young eating "team" ate fifty-two sandwiches at twenty-three stands in two states. The impact of the resulting piece on the top-ranked John's Roast Pork and Chink's Steaks was immediate and dramatic. John's had to get cops to direct traffic; Joseph Groh of Chink's remembers running out of bread every night for weeks afterward. The fact that LaBan's dining companions were just about to go away to college and away from cheesesteaks allowed the article to dig into some of the deeper reasons for the food's local hold.

It all added up to the "most well-read article I have ever written. It's been reposted umpteen times and has stood the test of time, at least when it comes to the best stands," LaBan says. And it's a good thing too. Because while LaBan says he expects to be writing about cheesesteaks for the rest of his Philadelphia food-writing career, he vows to "never again eat fifty-two cheesesteaks in four days."

THE OTHER WEB SITE

One of the two premiere cheesesteak sites on the Web was born over dinner in, yes, a *sushi* restaurant where Web site cofounder Andy Stein began raving about the cheesesteak lunch he had eaten at Chink's Steaks a few hours earlier. After discussing Chink's, Stein and friend Rob Rush agreed that there needed to be a cyberspace where people could review and rate the best local cheesesteak stands and other icons of Philadelphia pop culture. Besides a general knowledge of Greater Philly gained from growing up in the area, Stein had spent almost ten years checking out unfamiliar cheesesteak stands with his dad, which is what led him to Chink's that fateful day.

On the resulting cheesesteaktown.com Web site, which launched with the help of computer geek Kenny Fine in summer 2007, the cofounders write under the avatar aliases Ozzard of Whiz (Stein), Big Cheese (Rush), and Fried Onion (Fine). All the other characters on the site are fictional creations who spout cheesesteak stand opinions Stein and the others get from site visitors at a rate of about 2,400 per day.

Cheesesteaktown is also about the whole range of low-brow culture swirling around the cheesesteak. Accordingly, the site includes information about oddball local attractions (the Franklin Institute's giant heart and Fairmount Park's whispering bench) and celebrities (Massa the gorilla and kiddie show TV host Pixanne), as well as an online store that sells T-shirt tributes to the "Iggles" (that is, the Philadelphia Eagles football team), the famous Iggles fan Santa-booing incident, and amateur cartoonist Stein's Land of Whiz (where the streets are paved with Whiz instead of gold).

WIP'S ULTIMATE CHEESESTEAK CHALLENGE

"You've got a death wish," a friend warned WIP sports radio host Glen Macnow after Macnow announced plans to ferret out the best local cheesesteak by eating forty-five of them in as many days. That's not because of all the fat and cholesterol Macnow would be getting but because of all the listeners he would be offending. Macnow himself acknowledges that in Philly it's safer to "question a man's choice of women" or criticize his favorite sports team than to slam "his number one cheesesteak." So Macnow wasn't surprised when his spring 2008 steak shop forays generated three to four times the feedback as his prior-year judgings of local burger, rib, and pizza joints. Even more impressive than the number of phone calls and Web site postings was their vehemence. Here's a sampling:

> **"No Steaks on South! Are you kidding? S.O.S. has got to be a top 5 on this list yet it's not on at all. I'm a fat guy I would know."**

> "Glen, get your ass over to Lee's right now."

> **"Glen, I hope there is a reason I am not aware of for Philip's to not be on this list. It does not compute that Philip's did not make this list and Pat's did."**

> "Whoever wrote in saying that Duff's is better than Dalessandro's is seriously 'out there' and DOES NOT KNOW A THING about cheesesteaks."

"I was called an idiot more than once," Macnow readily admits. But he insists the positive feedback far outweighed the negative. "We didn't just go to all the icons and say they were great. In fact, some of the most famous places got quite low ratings. People appreciated our honesty."

Those in the "Glen is an idiot" camp got a chance to test out that theory at an on-air taste-off of Macnow's favorite six cheesesteaks conducted by members of the public and a panel of food, sports, and media celebrities that included five-star restaurant chef Georges Perrier and ex-Eagle Vince Papale and Ike Reese. Both sets of judges confirmed Macnow's top rating of John's Roast Pork and Chink's (although not his love of Steve's Prince of Steaks and Talk of the Town).

Even more important to Macnow than the ratings of cheesesteaks are the ratings for his show, which rose significantly during the six-week cheesesteak contest.

THE TV SCENE

The Fresh Prince of Bel-Air was an early to mid-1990s television show that starred Will Smith as a streetwise Philadelphian sent to live with his rich aunt and uncle in Los Angeles. In the fifth episode of the first season, Will's Uncle Phil tries to cheer up the homesick kid by buying him a cheesesteak from an L.A. café.

"Nice try, Uncle Phil, but this is not a Philadelphia cheesesteak. See, look at the bag. No grease stain. If this were an authentic Philadelphia cheesesteak, you could see right through the bag by now," Will says before going on to sing Pat's praises.

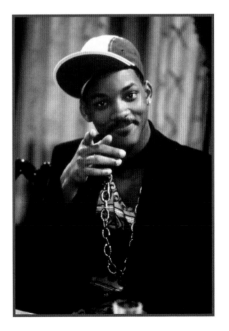

GLEN MACNOW'S TOP 10

1. John's Roast Pork
2. Steve's Prince of Steaks
3. Chink's
4. Talk of the Town
5. Grey Lodge Pub
6. Slack's
7. Sonny's
8. Tony Luke's
9. White House Sub
10. Dalessandro's

Glen Macnow (left) presided over the taste-off/broadcast.

CHAPTER 5:

DIY CHEESESTEAK

THE CHEESESTEAK IS MAINLY A RESTAURANT FOOD: ONE OF THE BEST THINGS ABOUT IT IS THAT YOU DON'T HAVE TO MAKE IT. BUT THIS POSITIVE CAN BECOME A NEGATIVE IF YOU CAN'T FIND A NEARBY JOINT THAT MAKES A GOOD ONE (EVEN AFTER CAREFUL STUDY OF CHAPTERS 2 AND 3). OR PERHAPS YOU LOVE THE CHEESESTEAK TASTE SO MUCH THAT YOU'D LIKE TO EXPERIENCE IT IN DIFFERENT FORMS. IF SO, THIS DIY CHAPTER IS FOR YOU.

THE ORIGINAL BASIC CHEESESTEAK

This basic recipe is courtesy of Pat's King of Steaks, the shop that started it all and has been doing it the longest. Note that Pat's serves the meat slab-style; it is not chopped in the manner of most places in Philadelphia and abroad. The King also does not follow the common practice of finishing off the onions on the grill with the meat. Anyone you make this recipe for who complains about this should be served last, as per Pat's traditional tough love.

Serves 4

1 (8-ounce) jar Cheese Whiz
6 tablespoons soybean oil, divided
1 large Spanish onion, coarsely chopped
1½ pounds rib-eye steak, thinly sliced (have the butcher slice it or slice it yourself, partially frozen)
4 crusty Italian rolls, split partially open lengthwise
Hot cherry peppers, for serving (optional)
Hot sauce, for serving (optional)
Ketchup, for serving (optional)

Melt the Whiz in a double boiler or microwave oven, stirring occasionally, until hot (but not boiling).

Heat a cast iron or nonstick skillet over medium heat. Add 3 tablespoons oil to the skillet, and sauté the onion until soft and golden, about 5 minutes. Remove the onion. Add the remaining 3 tablespoons oil to the skillet. Sauté the steak slices until brown on one side, about 1 minute, and then flip to the other side and repeat; do not chop the meat.

Place one-fourth of the steak into each roll. Divide the onion among the rolls and top with the hot cheese. Serve as desired with hot peppers, hot sauce, and ketchup.

Pat's Frank Olivieri Jr. puts on a finishing touch of Whiz.

ITALIAN ROLLS

Bread maker and teacher Peter Reinhart doesn't buy into the mystique of the Philadelphia hoagie roll. "I don't think the rolls in Philly are much different than those found in New York or Chicago or anywhere else. As long as it's fresh and properly made, not too hard and crusty, not too sweet, a little bit of chew to it with a nice balance of salt to sweetness, there are many brands that could work," he says.

Those who can't find that kind of a roll near their home might want to consider making their own using this recipe from Reinhart's award-winning *The Bread Baker's Apprentice*—not just because Reinhart obviously knows a lot about bread but because, having grown up in Penn Valley eating at Mama's and Larry's, he also knows a lot about the Italian rolls used to make cheesesteaks.

INGREDIENTS: Makes 9 hoagie rolls

3½ cups biga (recipe follows)
2½ cups unbleached bread flour
1⅔ teaspoons salt
1 tablespoon sugar
1 teaspoon active dry yeast
1 teaspoon diastatic barley malt powder (optional)
1 tablespoon olive oil, vegetable oil, or shortening
¾ cup to ¾ cup and 2 tablespoons lukewarm milk
(90 to 100°F)
Semolina flour or cornmeal for dusting

Remove the biga from the refrigerator 1 hour before making the dough. Cut it into about ten small pieces with a pastry scraper or serrated knife. Cover with a towel or plastic wrap and let sit for 1 hour to take off the chill.

Stir together the bread flour, salt, sugar, yeast, and malt powder in a large bowl (or in the bowl of an electric mixer). Add the biga pieces, oil, and ¾ cup milk, and stir together (or mix on low speed with the paddle attachment) until a ball forms, adjusting the milk or flour as needed. The dough should be slightly sticky and soft, but not batterlike or very sticky. If the dough feels tough and stiff, add more water to soften it (it is better to have the dough too stiff at this point).

Sprinkle flour on a work surface, transfer the dough to the counter, and begin kneading (or mixing on medium speed with the dough hook). Knead (or mix) for about 10 minutes, adding flour as needed, until the dough is tacky, but not sticky, and supple. The dough should register 77 to 81°F and pass the "windowpane test"—that is, if you cut a piece of dough off and stretch it out in your hand, it should hold a translucent, paper-thin membrane. If it does not, keep mixing. When it does, lightly oil a large bowl and transfer the dough to the bowl, rolling it to coat it with the oil. Cover the bowl with plastic wrap. Ferment at room temperature for approximately 2 hours, or until the dough redoubles in size.

Gently divide the dough into nine pieces of about 4 ounces each. Carefully form the pieces into rolls, degassing the dough as little as possible. Lightly dust with a sprinkle of flour, cover with a towel or plastic wrap, and let rest for 5 minutes. Shape each hoagie roll by gently flattening the measured piece of dough and folding in the sides to square it off. Roll it up and seal the crease like a bâtarde, creating surface tension. Rock and roll the dough into a torpedo shape, exerting extra pressure on the ends to taper the dough.

Line a baking sheet with parchment paper and dust with the semolina flour. Place the rolls on the baking sheet and lightly mist with cooking spray. Cover loosely with plastic wrap. Proof at room temperature for about 1 hour, or until the rolls have grown to about one and a half times their original size. Score the rolls with two parallel diagonal slashes or one long slash.

Place an empty cast iron skillet on the top rack of the oven or the oven floor, and preheat the oven to 500°F. Fill a clean plant mister with lukewarm water. Heat some water in a tea kettle. Once the oven is heated, place the sheet of rolls in the oven and immediately (and carefully) pour 1 cup simmering water from the kettle into the empty skillet (at an angle and using hot pads to avoid being burned) and quickly close the oven door. After 30 seconds, spray the side and back walls of the oven with the mister and close the door. Repeat once more after another 30 seconds. After the final spray, lower the oven setting to 450°F and bake for about 15 minutes, rotating 180 degrees, if necessary, for even baking. The rolls should be golden brown and register at least 200°F at the center.

Transfer the rolls or loaves to a cooling rack and cool for at least 1 hour before slicing or serving.

BIGA

INGREDIENTS: Makes about 3½ cups

2½ cups unbleached bread flour
½ teaspoon active dry yeast
¾ cup plus 2 tablespoons to 1 cup (7 to 8 ounces) water, at
room temperature

Stir together the flour and yeast in a large bowl (or in the bowl of an electric mixer). Add ¾ cup plus 2 tablespoons water, stirring until everything comes together and makes a coarse ball (or mix on low speed for 1 minute with the paddle attachment). Adjust the flour or water as needed, so that the dough is neither too sticky nor too stiff. (It is better to err on the sticky side, as you can adjust more easily during kneading. It is harder to add water once the dough firms up.)

Sprinkle some flour on a work surface and transfer the dough to the work surface. Knead for 4 to 6 minutes (or mix on medium speed with the dough hook for 4 minutes), or until the dough is soft and pliable, tacky but not sticky. The internal temperature should be 77 to 81°F.

Lightly oil a bowl and transfer the dough to the bowl, rolling it around to coat it with oil. Cover the bowl with plastic wrap and ferment at room temperature for 2 to 4 hours, or until it nearly doubles in size.

Remove the dough from the bowl, knead it slightly to degas, and return it to the bowl, covering the bowl with plastic wrap. Place the bowl in the refrigerator overnight. You can keep this in the refrigerator for up to 3 days, or freeze it in an airtight plastic bag for up to three months.

GRANNY DALESSANDRO'S LONG HOTS

The only thing at Dalessandro's more beloved than the onions are the long hots. A staple condiment at Philadelphia steak shops, they can be scarce elsewhere. That's why out-of-towners might find this recipe particularly handy. Some shops cook the peppers in the oven, but Fran Dalessandro Sack makes them on the stovetop like her grandmother Philomena, the recipe's inventor and namesake. Sack says the secret to good peppers is not overcooking.

INGREDIENTS: Makes enough for 8 sandwiches

15 long hot red or green peppers, stems removed, cut into
2- or 3-inch pieces
Olive or vegetable oil or a blend

Place the peppers in a medium skillet and add enough oil to reach half the depth of the pepper layer. Heat to medium-high. When the oil is hot, cover the skillet and lower the heat. Cook the covered peppers at a simmer, stirring occasionally, until the peppers are just starting to get soft, about 7 minutes. Remove the skillet from the heat. Let the covered skillet sit until the peppers are more cooked but still somewhat firm, about another 7 minutes. Drain off the oil with a strainer and top your sandwiches with the peppers. Leftover peppers can be stored in a covered container in the refrigerator for about 5 days.

Fran Sack prepares to tackle some long hots.

NEW CENTURY CHEESESTEAK

This is the rare cheesesteak that looks as good as it tastes. It won first prize in the Wyndham Franklin Plaza's Gourmet Cheesesteak Competition (see page 148) for chef Albert Paris, then of Rococo and now of Mantra, in late 1999— hence the New Century name. Serve these cheesesteaks with gaufrettes (waffle chips), or other fried potatoes or potato chips.

INGREDIENTS: Serves 6

SESAME BREAD
1 (¼-ounce) packet active dry yeast
2½ cups warm water (100°F), divided
2 tablespoons sugar
6½ cups all-purpose flour
2 tablespoons vegetable oil
2 teaspoons salt
1 egg, lightly beaten
Sesame seeds

CHEESESTEAK
3 pounds filet mignon
½ cup olive oil, divided
1 pound mushrooms, sliced
1 pound onions, sliced
8 ounces provolone cheese, shredded (about 2 cups)
1 teaspoon salt
2 teaspoons pepper

SAUCE
1 cup ketchup
2 tablespoons peeled, seeded, and chopped tomato
1 tablespoon honey
1 teaspoon red wine vinegar
2 tablespoons hot water

FOR THE ROLLS, mix the yeast in ¼ cup warm water in a small bowl and let rest for 10 minutes. In the bowl of an electric mixer, combine the yeast mixture, remaining water, sugar, flour, vegetable oil, and salt with a dough hook. Roll the dough into six rolls of about 6 ounces each. Let proof for 1 hour.

Preheat the oven to 350°F. Brush the rolls with egg and sprinkle with sesame seeds. Bake for 20 minutes or until golden brown; let rest until cool.

FOR THE CHEESESTEAK, rub the filet mignon with half the olive oil, and grill in a skillet over medium-high heat until medium rare. Remove from the skillet and slice as thinly as possible. Return the meat to the skillet with the rest of the olive oil. Add the mushrooms and onions, and cook until the meat is brown and the mushrooms and onions are soft. Add cheese to the skillet and toss. Add the salt and pepper. The mixture will be gooey.

FOR THE SAUCE, in a separate small skillet, mix the ketchup, tomato, honey, vinegar, and hot water. Simmer for 5 minutes. Put through a sieve.

TO SERVE, hollow out the rolls and fill with the steak mixture. Coat a plate with the sauce and serve the cheeseteaks on top.

Al Paris with his New Century award-winner

It sure doesn't look like a cheesesteak

CHEESESTEAK SOUP

There appear to be two major approaches to making cheesesteak into soup. One follows the lead of onion soup, with its beef stock base and broiled provolone; the other approach, of which the following recipe is an example, should appeal to people who like a little steak with their Whiz. It comes from Campbell's, whose corporate headquarters is located right across the Delaware River from Philadelphia in Camden, New Jersey, and so should know a thing or two about cheesesteaks.

INGREDIENTS: Serves 2 (3 cups)

2 (2-ounce) frozen sandwich steaks
2 tablespoons butter
1 medium onion, cut into thin wedges
½ small green bell pepper, cut into strips
1 (11-ounce) can Campbell's condensed cheddar cheese soup
1 cup water
1 teaspoon Worcestershire sauce
1½ cups toasted (1-inch) bread cubes

Cut each steak into 2 x ½-inch strips. Melt the butter in a large saucepan. Add the onion and green pepper and cook over medium heat until tender, stirring occasionally. Add the steak strips and cook just until the meat changes color, stirring often. Stir in the soup until smooth. Gradually stir in the water and Worcestershire sauce, and heat through. Serve the soup topped with the toasted bread cubes.

CHEESESTEAK PIZZA

Despite the large presence of Italians and Italian restaurants, Philadelphia is not really a pizza town. It's a cheesesteak one (in case you haven't already guessed). Every pizza shop sells cheesesteaks and a number also make cheesesteak pizza, Dolce Carini being among the best.

This recipe follows owner Mayuri Clune's general formula of steak, onion, and cheeses to create a cheese-and-meat-heavy white pizza. Dolce Carini sells it by the slice at lunch, if you're in town and want to sample it before making a whole pie (although most home chefs will find it a challenge to recreate the shop's wonderful chewy-crunchy crust).

INGREDIENTS: Serves 4

2 tablespoons vegetable oil
8 ounces rib-eye steak, thinly sliced, or frozen sandwich steak
1 medium onion, diced
1 large (12-inch) prepared pizza crust or dough
7 to 10 slices American cheese
2 ounces mozzarella cheese, shredded (about ½ cup)

Preheat the oven to 450°F. Heat the oil in a large skillet over medium-high heat. Add the onion and fry until soft. Add the steak and cook until brown, about 5 minutes, chopping the steak and mixing it with the onion.

Cover the pizza crust with the American cheese. Cover the cheese with the steak and onion mixture. Sprinkle the mozzarella cheese over it all. Bake the pizza for 12 minutes or until the cheese is melted and the crust is brown at the edges.

CHEESESTEAK CRÊPE

Pari has been feeding hungry University of Pennsylvania students from its original truck or current location inside UPenn's Houston Hall food court since the mid-1990s. But it has only been making its cheesesteak crêpe for the past two years. It was invented by stand worker Alfred Cani on a slow night and almost instantly became a top-five seller.

All crêpes at Pari come with brown gravy sauce and a standard grilled vegetable medley of mushrooms, tomatoes, spinach, broccoli, onions, and peppers unless otherwise requested. The recipe here calls for only the more traditional cheesesteak vegetables—onions, mushrooms, and peppers—but you can, of course, improvise with your own combination. Ready-made crêpes are available in gourmet stores (Frieda's is one brand) if you'd rather not make your own.

INGREDIENTS: Serves 3 to 4

CRÊPES

½ cup all-purpose flour
½ teaspoon salt
¾ cup low-fat milk
1 egg

CHEESESTEAK FILLING

3 tablespoons vegetable oil
1 pound rib-eye steak, thinly sliced, or frozen sandwich steak
1 large onion, diced
1 large green bell pepper, diced
6 ounces white mushrooms, diced (2½ to 3 cups)
8 slices white American cheese
1 tablespoon butter, melted
½ cup shredded mozzarella cheese or grated provolone cheese

For the crêpes, combine the flour, salt, milk, and egg in a blender pitcher and blend until smooth. (Or beat by hand in a bowl with a spout.) Refrigerate covered for at least 1 hour (or up to a day).

For the cheesesteak filling, briefly heat the oil in a large skillet. Add the onion, pepper, and mushrooms and fry until soft. Add the steak and cook until brown, about 5 minutes, chopping the steak and mixing it with the vegetables. Remove from the heat.

Take the batter out of the refrigerator and beat again. Place a small nonstick skillet over medium heat until a drop of water bubbles. Add the butter. Pour just enough batter to thinly cover the bottom of the pan when you pick up the pan and swirl it. (Pour the excess batter back into the bowl.) When the top is set, in less than 1 minute, turn the crêpe over with a spatula and cook until the bottom is slightly brown, no more than 20 seconds. Repeat, adjusting the heat as needed, until all the batter is used. Stack the finished crêpes on a plate.

Preheat the oven to 375°F. Place one finished crêpe on a flat surface. Place one American cheese slice in the center. Place about 4 tablespoons of the steak and vegetable mixture in the middle of the lower third and then roll it up. Place the crêpe, seam side down, on a greased ovenproof platter or baking dish. Repeat for the rest of the crêpes. When all the crêpes are on the platter, sprinkle with the mozzarella cheese. Bake uncovered for 10 to 12 minutes or until the cheese is melted and the crêpes are warmed through.

CHEESESTEAK PIEROGI

The Czerw family has been making smoked kielbasa and other Polish delicacies the same way since Polish émigré Jan Czerw converted the Port Richmond, Philadelphia, horse stable into a butcher shop in 1938. And while his descendants respect their culinary heritage, they are not totally bound by it. The shop's cheesesteak pierogi are a perfect example. Invented by Jan's grandson John, who now runs the business with his brothers Dennis and Jeffrey, they're especially popular with Eagles football tailgaters—for whom John will sometimes dye the pierogi cheesesteak dough Eagles green.

INGREDIENTS: Makes 5 dozen pierogi

FILLING

2 pounds frozen sandwich steak
Vegetable oil (optional)
1 medium onion, chopped (optional)
8 ounces American, provolone, or cheddar cheese, shredded (about 2 cups)

PIEROGI

5 cups all-purpose flour
6 egg yolks
3 eggs
1 teaspoon salt
¾ cup water
¼ pound (1 stick) butter

For the filling, fry the steak in 1 tablespoon oil in a large skillet over medium-high heat, as you would to make a cheesesteak. Let cool. Using a food processor, pulse a small amount of the steak until it is finely chopped. Transfer to a large mixing bowl. Repeat until all the steak is chopped. If using onions, heat 1 tablespoon oil in a skillet over medium-high heat and sauté until slightly brown. Mix the onions with the steak. Mix in the shredded cheese.

For the pierogi, in a large bowl make a mound out of the flour and make a well in the center. Place the egg yolks and eggs in the center. Cut in the flour with a knife and add the salt and water. Knead until firm. Cut into three equal parts. On a floured surface, roll out one of the dough parts thinly, to about 1/8-inch thickness (see note). Cut 3-inch circles with a glass or cookie/biscuit cutter. Put the other two pieces of dough in a plastic bag to keep them from drying out.

Place a small ball of filling, about 1 tablespoon, on each dough circle. Moisten the edge of each circle with water. For each circle, fold the dough over, forming a semicircle. Press the edges together with the tines of a fork or by pressing firmly with your fingers. Repeat the whole process for the other two pieces of dough.

Boil a large pot of water, about 2 gallons, seasoned with about a teaspoon of salt. Gently slide twelve pierogi into the water. Don't let the water boil too vigorously while cooking the pierogi—just boil gently. Cook until they float to the top, about 8 to 10 minutes. Meanwhile, fill two medium bowls with cold water.

Once the pierogi are done, gently take them out with a large slotted spoon and place them into one bowl of cold water. Then immediately gently transfer the same twelve pierogi into the second bowl of cold water. Let them sit until your next group of pierogi has cooked, and then put the cooled pierogi into a colander to drain. (There is no need to refill the bowls of cold water for the different batches.) Keep repeating this process until all the pierogi are boiled and cooled.

Melt some of the butter in a skillet on medium heat and gently sauté the pierogi in batches. Cook until each is slightly brown on one side and turn them over. Continue cooking until the other side is slightly brown.

NOTE: Beginners might find it easier to roll the dough out thinly by cutting off 1-inch cubes of dough and rolling out each pierogi circle individually.

CHEESESTEAK, NO STARCH

Everybody knows that you can make grilled cheese sandwiches with an iron (at least, everyone who has read my *Kitchen Sink Cookbook: Offbeat Recipes from Unusual Ingredients* does). The idea to use the same method to cook sandwich steak comes from a college student who once told Steak-umm executive Eugene Gagliardi Jr. that he ironed the product to get around his school's ban on dormitory cooking appliances.

INGREDIENTS: Serves 1

2 slices (3 to 4 ounces) frozen sandwich steak
½ small onion, thinly sliced so that the rings separate (about ¼ cup)
3 slices American cheese
1 (9-inch) Italian roll, partially split

Preheat the iron to medium-high. Wrap one steak slice and half the onion rings in two sheets of heavy-duty aluminum foil with generous seams to prevent leakage and future beefy-smelling clothes. Repeat for the second slice.

Place a towel on an ironing board. Put the wrapped steak on the towel and then place the iron on the sandwich. *Do not at any time leave the iron or the packets unattended.* Lift the iron up after 45 seconds, flip the packet, and repeat on the other side. Repeat until you can smell the meat and onions cooking, around 3 minutes. Carefully peel back the hot foil. If the meat is warm and brown and the onions are soft, close this packet and set it aside. (If the contents are not done, repeat until they are.)

Repeat the process with the other foil packet. As soon as the second packet is cooked, open it up, cover that slice of meat with the cheese slices, and seal the foil back up for about 1 minute or until the cheese is warm but not runny.

Unwrap both foil packets, place the onions and steaks in the roll, and eat.

NOTE: If you prefer chopped-style steak, chop the onion-topped meat on a plate or cutting board with a spatula or knife before placing in the roll.

CHEESESTEAK OMELET

To paraphrase a beloved White Castle hamburger advertising campaign: Cheesesteak for breakfast? Why not?

INGREDIENTS: Serves 1

1 tablespoon butter
1 (1½- to 2-ounce) serving frozen sandwich steak or similar amount of rib-eye steak, thinly sliced
2 teaspoons chopped onion
3 eggs
2 slices American or provolone cheese
Salt and pepper to taste
Italian bread (optional)

Melt half the butter in a nonstick 8-inch skillet on medium-high heat. Add the steak and onion and cook until the steak is brown, 2 to 3 minutes. Transfer to a plate.

Beat the eggs in a bowl with a whisk. Heat the skillet on high and add the remaining butter. Add the eggs all at once. After the bottom sets, in about 30 seconds, put a spatula under one side of the eggs and tilt the pan so that the loose egg fills the empty spot. Continue doing that around the pan until no uncooked egg is left on top. Place the cheese and the steak filling across the middle of the omelet. Fold the thicker side over to create a half-moon. Remove from the heat and season with salt and pepper. Serve with toasted slices of Italian bread to complete the pseudocheesesteak effect.

CHEESESTEAK SPRING ROLLS

Cheesesteak egg rolls and the more delicate spring rolls abound in Greater Philly. But this Four Seasons hotel version is the only one to make *Saveur* magazine's 100 list (in 2006) and, what's perhaps even more important to locals, score a 4.5 out of a possible 5 in *Philadelphia* magazine's 2004 One Man, 50 Cheesesteaks survey.

INGREDIENTS: Serves 1

2 tablespoons olive oil
5 ounces frozen sandwich steak meat
2 slices American cheese
1 slice provolone cheese
Salt and pepper to taste
2 spring roll wrappers (available in the freezer section of Asian supermarkets)
2 egg yolks, beaten
3 cups soybean oil
Ketchup, for garnish
2 banana peppers, for garnish
Freshly made potato chips or fried shoestring potatoes, for garnish (optional)

The Four Seasons' Cheesesteak Spring Rolls

Heat the olive oil in a medium sauté pan. Add the steak and cook through while chopping vigorously, approximately 4 minutes. Remove any grease or fat from the pan. Add the American and provolone cheeses. Lower the heat and mix well. Add the salt and pepper. Allow to cool.

Cover one of the spring roll wrappers with a damp towel. Brush the other wrapper with enough egg yolk to cover the entire wrapper. Place the cheesesteak mixture on one end of that wrapper. Form and roll into a log shape. Place the other wrapper in a diamond shape and brush the corners with yolk. Place the filled log on the center of the second wrap, and enclose the filled log in the other wrap by folding in the sides, brushing the edges with egg yolk, and sealing with your fingers.

Fill a deep fryer with soybean oil set to 350°F. Carefully place the two-layered spring roll in the center and cook until golden brown, about 4 minutes.

Cut the roll diagonally into four pieces. Garnish with ketchup and banana peppers and, if desired, freshly made potato chips or fried shoestring potatoes.

CHEESESTEAK CASSEROLE

If there were a cheesesteak recipe popularity contest, the cheesesteak casserole would win it. A quick Google search yields dozens of hits. Some are cooked in a skillet, one is Mexican-themed, another has twenty-nine ingredients. (No cheesesteak recipe should have twenty-nine ingredients, *especially* not a casserole.) This version sticks to tradition and the basic cheesesteak casserole formula of meat, pasta, and cheese.

INGREDIENTS: Serves 4 to 6

8 ounces of your favorite uncooked pasta (bow-tie, elbow, egg noodle, etc.)
Salt and pepper to taste
1½ pounds ground beef
2 medium onions, chopped (about 1 cup)
2 garlic cloves, finely chopped
1 green bell pepper, chopped (about ¼ cup)
1 (14-ounce) can beef broth
¼ cup all-purpose flour
½ cup light cream
3 tablespoons butter, melted
1 cup dry Italian breadcrumbs
4 ounces American cheese, shredded (about 1 cup)

Preheat the oven to 350°F. Cook and drain the pasta according to the package directions.

Add salt and pepper to the ground beef and place in a large nonstick skillet over medium heat. Cook the beef, stirring constantly, until no longer pink, about 2 minutes. Add the onions, garlic, and pepper and cook until they begin to soften, about 3 minutes. Spoon the beef and vegetable mixture into a greased 2-quart (11 x 7-inch) baking dish.

Whisk the broth and flour together in a small bowl until smooth. Add to the same (unwashed) skillet and heat to boiling. Cook, stirring constantly, until it thickens. Remove from the heat and let cool about 10 minutes. Stir in the cream. Pour the cream mixture over the beef mixture in the baking dish. Stir in the cooked noodles.

Cover with foil and bake. Meanwhile, combine the melted butter and breadcrumbs in a medium bowl, and mix in the shredded cheese. When the casserole has cooked for 40 minutes, take it out of the oven, uncover it, and spread the cheese and breadcrumb mixture evenly over the top. Bake uncovered for an additional 10 minutes or until the cheese is melted and the casserole bubbles.

CHEESESTEAK SALAD

This dish is served by a surprising number of pizza and steak shops, most of them outside Philadelphia. The Atkins diet is to blame. Most places offer the traditional ranch, French, and Italian salad dressing options, but Dimitri's International Grille in suburban Baltimore developed this Cherry Pepper Dressing specifically for its cheesesteak salad.

INGREDIENTS: Serves 4

6 tablespoons vegetable oil
1 large onion, coarsely chopped
1½ pounds rib-eye steak, thinly sliced, or 1 (28-ounce) box frozen sandwich steak
8 thin slices provolone cheese
1 (10-ounce) bag torn romaine lettuce
½ to 1 cup Cherry Pepper Dressing (recipe follows)

Heat the oil in a large skillet over medium-high heat. Add the onion and fry until soft. Add the steak and cook until brown, about 5 minutes, chopping the steak and mixing it with the onion. Remove the pan from the heat. Place the cheese on top of the hot meat, and cover the pan until the cheese melts, about 1 minute.

Divide the lettuce among four plates. Top each plate of lettuce with a quarter of the meat and cheese mixture. Drizzle with the dressing and serve.

CHERRY PEPPER DRESSING

INGREDIENTS: Makes 1 cup

½ cup chopped hot cherry peppers
½ teaspoon balsamic vinegar
½ cup mayonnaise
3 teaspoons honey
¼ cup extra virgin olive oil

Place the peppers, vinegar, mayonnaise, and honey in a blender and process for 1 minute. While the blender is running, very slowly pour in the oil and blend until well mixed.

FRIED CHEESESTEAK

Yes, there is something worse, nutritionally speaking, than a cheesesteak or even a Philly taco (see page 75). That would be the deep-fried cheesesteak served at pizza shops in Lowell, Massachusetts, and Baltimore, Maryland. Suppa's Pizza and Subs of Lowell has been making its signature Steak Stick since 2004; Hot Tomatoes in Baltimore since 2006. Both roll a traditional steak topping up in pizza dough (rather than Italian bread), then drop it into a deep fryer. Mark Dayton of Hot Tomatoes says his customers have likened the resulting sandwich to a Mexican chimichanga or a cheesesteak doughnut.

INGREDIENTS: Serves 1 to 2

Vegetable oil
16 ounces pizza dough
10 ounces frozen sandwich steak
6 ounces mozzarella or provolone cheese or a combination, shredded (about 1½ cups)
Ranch dressing, for serving (optional)

Fill a deep fryer with oil and preheat to 350°F. Roll the pizza dough out in a 12-inch circle on a work surface.

Place the steak and 2 tablespoons oil in a skillet. Cook over medium-high heat, chopping the meat as it cooks, for about 5 minutes or until just before the meat turns completely brown.

Sprinkle the pizza dough with half the cheese. Spread the cooked steak over the cheese. Sprinkle with the rest of the cheese. In your mind's eye, divide the pizza circle into thirds with parallel lines. Fold the right and left thirds over the center, enclosing the filling. Seal the edges with your fingers. Roll the whole thing up like you would a bedroll.

Place the steak stick in the fryer, and fry until it turns a crispy golden brown, about 10 to 15 minutes. Serve with ranch dressing.

PHILLY CHEESEFAKE

If Benjamin Franklin is the old face of Philadelphia, then Elizabeth Fiend—she of the jeweled cat's-eye glasses, Pippi Longstocking duds, and 1965 Schwinn "wheels"—is the new.

As hostess of local public access TV show *Big Tea Party* (which can be seen nationally on the satellite Dish Network's Free Speech TV), Fiend is an anarchist Martha Stewart. Martha would probably drop her linen napkin mid-hemstitch if she saw her alternative alter ego making a candelabra out of plastic soda bottles, dispensing advice on putting out your own CD, telling viewers how to avoid bicycle flats, and preparing a vegetarian Philly cheesesteak, or Philly Cheese*fake* as Fiend's husband, Allen, cleverly named it. Fiend says this is her most popular recipe as well as one of her least healthy. She also says that thin slicing of the specified ingredients is crucial to its taste.

INGREDIENTS: Serves 4

1 pound seitan or wheat meat (available at natural food stores), rinsed in a colander and very thinly sliced
1 large green bell pepper, very thinly sliced
1 large red bell pepper, very thinly sliced
1 large onion, very thinly sliced
1 tablespoon soy sauce
3 tablespoons ketchup
6 cloves garlic, finely chopped
1 tablespoon dried sage
1 or 2 dashes cayenne pepper
Olive oil or olive oil cooking spray
8 slices vegan cheese (or, "to get the most authentic flavor, the cheapest, most orange American cheese you can find,"says Fiend)
4 long sandwich (hoagie) rolls, whole wheat if available, split lengthwise

Preheat the oven to 400°F. Combine the sliced seitan, peppers, and onion in a bowl. Add the soy sauce, ketchup, garlic, sage, and cayenne pepper and mix again.

Lightly grease a baking sheet with olive oil, or spray with olive oil cooking spray. Spread the seitan mixture on the baking sheet and bake for 15 minutes. Turn the ingredients all around (while doing the Hokey Pokey, Elizabeth says), and bake for another 15 minutes. Take the pan out of the oven and shape the "meat" on the tray into four "steaks" the size of the rolls. Top with the onions, peppers, and cheese and put back into the oven just until the cheese melts. Place the cheese-covered "steaks" in the rolls and serve.

Elizabeth Fiend with her Philly Cheesefake

CHEESESTEAK EMPANADAS

We've already talked about the ubiquitous cheesesteak spring roll or egg roll appetizer. Good Dog Bar executive chef Jessica O'Donnell looked to Spanish cuisine for her gastropub's fried cheesesteak-flavored appetizer, which is, despite the bar's name and canine decor, no dog. In fact, when O'Donnell briefly took it off the menu in late 2007, customers howled almost as loudly as the bar's chocolate Lab inspiration, Dylan.

INGREDIENTS: Serves 4

16 frozen disco wrappers, thawed (Goya brand is available in most Mexican specialty shops)
8 ounces rib-eye steak, thinly sliced
Salt and pepper to taste
3 ounces sharp cheddar cheese, shredded (about ¾ cup)
1 teaspoon white truffle oil
1 egg, well beaten
Canola oil

Let the discos sit at room temperature just until thawed. Trim the discos to 4-inch circles using a 4-inch ring mold.

In a large heavy-bottomed skillet, sauté the steak with salt and pepper on medium-high heat, chopping constantly to break it up, until it is cooked through, about 10 mintues. Let the meat cool. Mix in the cheese and truffle oil. Adjust the seasoning as needed.

Place one disco wrapper on an empanada or pierogi press if available. If not, just place it on a flat surface. Fill the center of the disco with about 2 tablespoons of meat filling. (Be careful to keep the meat in the center area and not let it out to the edges). Brush the edges with a little egg and close the press very tight to seal the edges. If not using a press, use your thumb and forefinger to press the edges together very tightly. Repeat until you have filled all the disco wrappers.

Fill a deep fryer with oil and preheat to 320°F (see note). Deep-fry the empanadas in a fryer basket four to six at a time. Do not crowd the fryer basket. Place a second fryer basket on top of the one holding the empanadas to keep them submerged in the oil. Cook until the empanadas are light golden brown, about 3 to 5 minutes. Repeat until you have fried all the empanadas. Let the empanadas drain for a minute either in the fryer basket or on a paper towel. Serve immediately.

NOTE: If you do not have a deep fryer, you can fill a wide saucepan with at least 3 inches of oil.

THE SCHMITTER®

McNally's Tavern is so old (1927) and is so well known in the tony Philadelphia almost-suburb of Chestnut Hill that it's marked by a bench and a coach light rather than a sign. It's especially famous for this cheesesteak variation that Hugh McNally fashioned from a bunch of stuff he had on hand one night in the 1960s and served to a regular who was a Schmidt's beer drinker (hence, the name).

INGREDIENTS: Serves 1

1½ tablespoons olive oil or butter
4 to 5 ounces (3 to 4 very thin slices) bottom round beef
½ medium onion, thinly sliced
2 to 3 slices cooked salami (not Genoa)
3 slices white American cheese
2 to 3 slices fresh, ripe tomato
1 large kaiser roll, sliced in half lengthwise
Schmitter° Sauce or substitute (see note)

Preheat the broiler. Place the oil in a very hot large greased skillet or griddle, and cook the beef, onion, and salami side by side. After the beef is brown on one side, in 3 to 4 minutes, flip it and place the onion on top of the cooked side. Don't flip the salami; instead allow it to slightly blacken on one side. After that has happened, in about 3 to 4 more minutes, place one slice of cheese on the salami and top with the tomato slices. Continue to cook until the cheese melts.

Meanwhile, slightly melt a slice of cheese over each kaiser half in the broiler.

Now flip the salami-cheese-tomato stack onto the beef and onion so that the blackened side of the salami is on top. Place the entire beef-onion-tomato-cheese-salami stack on top of the melted cheese on the broiled roll bottom. Add sauce to taste, top with the other roll half, and serve.

NOTE: Schmitter° Sauce is available at www.mcnallystavern.com. Alternatively, you can use Russian or Thousand Island dressing, or you can make your own sauce by combining two parts mayonnaise, one part ketchup, and one-half part relish.

FREEZER KING

Pat Olivieri may have invented the cheesesteak, but if it weren't for Steak-umm, it would be about as famous as Rhode Island coffee syrup or South Carolina benne wafers (that is, virtually unknown by anybody not from there).

The story of America's most famous brand of boxed frozen sandwich steak is also the rags-to-riches story of Eugenio Gagliardi, an Italian immigrant with no money or English whose mid-1920s West Philly butcher shop grew into a meat-processing business that sold for $20 million in 1980. At various points along that stupendous rise, Gagliardi and his family supplied chicken to KFC and hamburgers to McDonald's. But Steak-umm was the company's sizzling success.

Other Philly area meat companies had begun molding and slicing steak for steak sandwiches in the 1950s. But these were whole beef fillets being sold to Philly area steak restaurants. Gagliardi Brothers was among the first to figure out how to fashion so-called sandwich or minute steaks out of smaller, cheaper cuts of meat and market them aggressively to supermarket shoppers on radio and TV. Steak-umm was advertised as the "60 second hot meal" and "the clean bite steak," a reference to the way processing eliminated (or hid) gristle.

Eugenio's son, Eugene Gagliardi Jr., the technical wizard behind the product, says the unusual name emerged on a road trip with his brother and a friend just after the product had been invented. Fed up with the brothers' unending name brainstorming, the friend finally spat out, "F—k 'em, stick 'em with Steak-umm."

Consumer advertising was backed up by store visits that doubled as cooking demonstrations. "To sell it out of the area, you had to put it into people's mouths," recalls Eugene's brother, Ralph, who handled company sales. "I brought my own grill and Amoroso rolls and cooked at the sales meetings." In fact, Ralph believes that early pairing is what started that bread company on the path to its now booming out-of-state frozen bread business. Whatever the causes of the cheesesteak's increased popularity, there's no question that the Gagliardis' Steak-umm efforts immeasurably raised the cheesesteak's profile across the country.

Eugenio Gagliardi did not patent his son's invention and so Steak'umm soon had many competitors. Today Steak'umm is one of five freezer-case minute steak brands owned by former competitor Quaker Maid of suburban Reading, Pennsylvania.

So what's the difference between Quaker Maid's Steak-umm, The Philly Steak, Philly-Gourmet, Philly Homestyle, and Quaker Maid brand chopped, formed sandwich steaks? "They're all probably pretty much the same thing," Eugene Gagliardi says in what could be seen as seller's remorse if this opinion weren't backed up by the products' identical nutritional labels and a Quaker Maid customer rep.

What's surprising is this processed steak pioneer's answer to the question of what kind of sandwich steak he would rather eat. "A piece of rib-eye from the butcher is always going to be preferable to any chopped and reformed product like Steak'umm," Gagliardi says.

ONION ADVICE

Many shops go through hundreds of pounds of onions daily to make their cheesesteaks "with." If anyone should know how to avoid crying while peeling and cutting them, the people who work there should. Here are a few of their ideas.

- **"Keep the onions cold and work fast." —Stephen Bledsoe of Dakota Pizza Company**

- **"Wash your hands with lemon juice or wear rubber gloves." —Joe Groh of Chink's Steaks**

- **"Don't touch your eyes." —Jack Mullan of Leo's**

- **"Wait it out. The crying danger is worst in the first few minutes when the onion skins come off and the juices are released. But it doesn't last." —Charles Alba of Lou's**

And if *you* have any ideas about how to get the smell of grilled onions out of your hair and clothes, these steak shop owners would love to hear from you.

An employee at Steve's Prince of Steaks tackles an unpopular task.

INDEX: PAGE REFERENCES FOR ILLUSTRATIONS ARE ITALICIZED.

the great
Philly
Cheesesteak
book